American Cultural
Baggage

American Cultural Baggage

How to Recognize and Deal with It

Stan Nussbaum

Illustrated by
Kathleen Webb

ORBIS BOOKS

Maryknoll, New York 10545

Copyright © 2005 by Stan Nussbaum.

Published by Orbis Books, Maryknoll, NY 10545-0308.

Manufactured in the United States of America.

Library of Congress Cataloging-in-Publication Data
Nussbaum, Stan.
    American cultural baggage : how to recognize and deal with it / Stan Nussbaum ; illustrated by Kathleen Webb.
        p. cm.
    ISBN-13: 978-1-57075-625-2 (pbk.)
    1. National characteristics, American. 2. Social values – United States.
3. Conduct of life. 4. United States – Civilization – Miscellanea.
5. Culture conflict – Miscellanea. I. Title.
E169.1 .N8155
306'.0973 – dc22

                                                        2005010667

Dedicated to
Milo and Violet Nussbaum,
the two Americans who made me one

Contents

Preface for Americans

As long as you live in the United States, you can get along very well without being conscious of your own culture. You automatically do things in an American way, and it automatically works.

When you go into another cultural setting, it doesn't work so well. You suddenly discover that you have unconsciously brought a lot of cultural baggage with you, and it is always causing trouble. You get angry with people because they do not measure up to expectations you didn't even know you had. You get laughed at or avoided for doing things in a normal American way without even thinking.

Even calling yourself an "American" can be controversial. We use the term in this book as convenient shorthand for citizens of the United States of America, but if you go north to Canada or south to Latin America, you are likely to hear that people don't think the United States owns the term. They'll let you use it, of course, because they recognize how clumsy "United Statesian" would be, but they may resent it.

The aim of this book is to help open your eyes to your own American culture. Then you can deal with it in a conscious way, choosing when to act American and when not to.

Throughout this book watch for the dynamite symbol. The paragraphs following the symbol are addressed to you as an American, explaining how a particular American cultural value can cause you trouble if you are unaware of it.

Becoming aware of our own culture is not quite as easy as it sounds. It has been said that as a fish would be the last creature to discover water, so the members of a particular culture would be the last ones to become conscious of it.

Culture is to a society what personality is to an individual — unconsciously built in, hard to describe, but easier to deal with once a person deliberately reflects on it. This book is a reflector, a mirror helping you to see what you look like to other people.

....

Preface for Everyone
Except Americans

....

This book helps people recognize and deal with American cultural baggage. You probably need no help recognizing it. It is already painfully obvious from your perspective, as you see Americans and their culture overrunning the whole planet these days. You see them charging into your country, making their typical American blunders. They are clueless about your culture and their own, and mystified when people are offended by their American ways. They need this book, though most don't know it — you may have to give them a copy!

Since many Americans do not deal with their own cultural baggage, the people around them are forced to deal with it. A clearer picture of American cultural values may help you. This book tries to draw the picture for you.

The aim here is neither to promote American culture nor attack it, but only to sketch it as clearly as possible. The sketch is based on 235 common sayings, grouped in this book around basic American cultural values.

Of course, no sketch gives a complete picture of a culture, especially not a large and complex one like America's. My observations on American culture are probably more accurate for white Americans than others, more for small towns than urban areas, more for the Midwest than other regions, more for the baby boomer generation than the younger generations, and more for men than women.

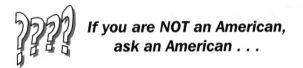

If you are NOT an American, ask an American . . .

To help you understand the particular Americans around you, some "Ask an American" questions are provided at the end of each short section. These are all marked by the symbol above. Most Americans will find these questions interesting but not threatening. A reading list is also provided for you at the end.

Note for International Students

You may prefer the shorter edition of this book, *Why Are Americans Like That? A Visitor's Guide to American Cultural Values and Expectations* (Colorado Springs, Colo.: Enculturation Books, 2005; available from www.enculturation.org). Only one hundred proverbs are included, footnotes explain the more difficult words, the explanations of cultural values are shorter, and the "DANGER" sections for American readers are left out. Whichever edition you choose, may it help you deal well with the Americans in your world.

Acknowledgments

First and foremost I need to thank the people of Lesotho and England. By living among them for several years, I was changed from a monocultural person into a tricultural one and given a vantage point from which to write this book.

Global Mapping International has allocated some of my working time to this project. Many thanks to my boss, Mike O'Rear, and other colleagues who regularly put up with the "Gone Writin'" sign on my office door.

The book was greatly improved by stacks of suggestions from relatives, friends, and acquaintances. These include Americans Adam, Carole, and Milo Nussbaum; Anjila Sisler, Evelyn Tomlin, David Hembroff, Norm Harpole, Bill Morrison, Alisa Lawrence, Kathy Lannon, Mark Patterson, Loren Muehlius, and Phil Cole, as well as advisers who look at American culture from the outside: Timothy Mambo (Congo), Gerrit and Celeste Wolfaardt (South Africa), Cesar Arroyo (Ecuador), Valerie Lim (Singapore), Wolfgang Mieder (Germany), Sabine Bofane-Decloedt (Belgium), Jane Law and Paul Message (Britain).

Special thanks to Suzanne Schorsch, who both prepared the work for publication and contributed some very helpful suggestions on its content. Final stages of the writing were done at the "Solitude Center," a tiny A-frame cabin on the grounds of the Rocky Mountain Mennonite Camp just below the western slopes of Pikes Peak. It is hard to imagine a finer place to think.

Chapter One

The "Ten Commandments" of American Culture

....

Here are ten very common sayings that will help you understand ten key American cultural values. I call them the "Ten
Commandments of American Culture" even though they are
not really "commandments." They have no religious or moral
authority like the Ten Commandments of the Bible do for
Jews and Christians. However, if you break any of these "cultural commandments," many Americans might think you do
not fit very well in America. This book will help you avoid the
problem by learning to understand American expectations.
(Note that when these commandments appear throughout the
rest of this book, a check mark appears along with them.)

While you are learning about American values, some of
your American friends may also want to learn about the values
of your own country. Please do discuss these things with us. If
you can help us understand you better, you enrich our lives.

✓ Commandment 1. You can't argue with success. (Be a success.)

Success is probably the highest value in American life.
It relates to so many other characteristics of American

life — individualism, freedom, goal-setting, progress, exper-
imenting, social mobility, making money, pragmatism, and
optimism.

Americans want to "make a success of themselves." This
is the "American Dream" that has attracted millions of im-
migrants and has been taught to generations of American
children. Everyone wants to be a success at something. If you
do not think that way, you may be considered a failure.

It is almost impossible to criticize success. For example, if
an employee does something without properly consulting his
supervisor, and as a result the company gets a big contract
with a new customer, the employee will get much more praise
than blame. The success of getting the new contract may be
more important than the failure to consult a superior.

Sometimes people will even say cheating is justified if it
brings success. Other people, however, may disagree.

*For more details about success, including a cartoon and
some "Ask an American" questions, go to page 22.*

☑ Commandment 2. Live and let live. (Be tolerant.)

Americans love freedom and privacy. In a way, that means we
love to be left alone. We don't want anyone interfering in our
affairs, giving us advice, or trying to run our lives. We want
people to "stay off our backs," "stay out of our way," and
"mind their own business."

Perhaps *Live and let live* should be listed as the first commandment of American culture, even more important than
success. It means that no one should object to anyone else's
way of living. If you like opera and I like country music, that

is fine. If you want to get married and I want to live with someone without marrying her, that is fine too. Neither of us should try to influence the other or object to the way the other lives.

If we are not tolerant of other people, we may damage their self-esteem. To attack someone's self-esteem is to break one of the most basic rules of American life.

For more details about tolerance and self-esteem, including a cartoon and some "Ask an American" questions, go to page 37.

✓ Commandment 3. Time flies when you're having fun. (Have lots of fun.)

Americans try to have as much fun as possible. Much of our fun comes through various kinds of entertainment, especially TV. But we also try to turn other activities into fun. Shopping is fun. Eating is fun, and in case it is not enough fun, we will put a playground inside the fast-food restaurant so the kids can have fun playing while the grown-ups have fun sitting and eating. Learning to read can be turned into fun, as the *Sesame Street* TV program shows. Americans look for careers that are fun (although not many succeed). Having fun is the major preoccupation of youth, retired people, and many of those in between.

In most situations Americans are very time-conscious. However, we forget to watch the clock when we are having fun. That is why "time flies," that is, time seems to go by very quickly.

For more details about fun, including a cartoon and some "Ask an American" questions, go to page 43.

☑ Commandment 4. Shop till you drop.

Many Americans (especially American women) shop as a form of recreation. Even if we are not shopping for anything in particular, we simply enjoy looking at all the options. We love the whole process of choosing what to buy and where to buy it. It is a major topic of social conversation. If you want to impress an American friend, convince him or her that you are a "smart shopper."

The saying *Shop till you drop* is never used seriously as a command and yet it holds a serious meaning. We are perhaps the ultimate consumer society, and this saying describes us so well that it could be our national motto.

For more details about choices, including a cartoon and some "Ask an American" questions, go to page 49.

☑ Commandment 5. Just do it.

We are people of action. We do not like too much planning. That seems indecisive and perhaps a waste of time. We do not like rules and regulations that prevent action. We strongly dislike authority structures where people are expected to inform several other people before they do anything. We get an idea, and we want to *just do it*.

Action is seen as the key to success. Action is more valuable than planning, checking regulations, or informing people.

For more details about initiative, including a cartoon and some "Ask an American" questions about initiative, go to page 69.

☑ Commandment 6. You are only young once. (Do whatever you can while you have the chance.)

This commandment ties together the themes of several other commandments — freedom, fun, initiative, and time. It is a command to enjoy life to the full, taking advantage of every opportunity that comes along. For example, this is why lots of university students flock to the Florida beaches for spring break, but the forty-year-olds don't. Adult responsibilities and schedules put an end to the freedom of youth.

For more details about youth and age, including a cartoon and some "Ask an American" questions, go to page 83.

☑ Commandment 7. Enough is enough. (Stand up for your rights.)

Human rights and dignity are so basic to American thinking that we assume everyone else must think the same way. This proverb implies the command, "Stand up for your rights." In the American Revolution, America as a nation said to Britain, *Enough is enough*, that is, "You have ruled us for long enough. You will not rule us anymore."

As we saw in Commandment 2, *Live and let live*, Americans do not want people interfering in their lives. When we sense interference, we push it away.

For more details about justice, including a cartoon and some "Ask an American" questions, go to page 104.

✓ Commandment 8. Rules are made to be broken. (Think for yourself.)

We obey rules most of the time, but we see rules as some-one else's idea of how we should do things. We think the rule might have been appropriate in some other situation, but it might not be appropriate for our situation now. Therefore, we break it and do what we think is a better idea. This proverb implies the commandment, "Think for yourself in every situation. Do not just obey rules."

Though Americans say, *Rules are made to be broken*, we never say, "Laws are made to be broken." Laws are official, legal "rules," and we proudly claim that in America, "No one is above the law."

For more details about rules, including a cartoon and some "Ask an American" questions, go to page 114.

✓ Commandment 9. Time is money. (Don't waste time.)

We Americans are very time-conscious and very money-conscious. Many of us get paid by the hour for the work we do. We give the employer our time in order to get money.

The idea that *time is money* has gotten into our minds so deeply that it affects our whole lives. Wasting time is as bad as wasting money, so we schedule everything and we hurry everywhere. We often signal the end of a phone conversation or a meeting by saying, "Well, I don't want to take up any more of your time."

If you really want to annoy an American, sit down and talk as if you have nothing else to do for the rest of the day.

You will be breaking the Ninth Commandment of American culture, "Don't waste time."

For more details about time, including a cartoon and some "Ask an American" questions, go to page 124.

☑ Commandment 10. God helps those who help themselves. (Work hard.)

In a list of "Ten Commandments," one might expect that God would be mentioned in the first commandment rather than the last one. But in American culture, God actually does come at the end of the list. For most Americans, God is much less a concern than success, money, and time. (There are many Americans who put God at the top of their personal list of priorities, but they are a minority within American culture.)

God helps those who help themselves could mean, "God rewards people who work hard," or it could mean, "God doesn't really help anyone. Your success depends on you, not God." Either way, the proverb points to the same commandment, "Whether you believe in God or not, work as hard as you can." It is better to be independent than to depend on other people.

For more details about God, including a cartoon and some "Ask an American" questions, go to page 139.

Chapter Two

The Top Priority in American Life

....

Since American life is goal-oriented from start to finish, let us begin our study of American culture by looking at three basic goals — being a success, building self-esteem, and having fun.

Individual Success

Americans are famous for being individualists. When we Americans think of success, we naturally think first of individual success. More than anything else in life, we want our biography to be a success story.

Success as an ideal

1. *You can't argue with success (Commandment 1).*
   Though you may tell someone they are doing something in a wrong way, you have to stop criticizing them if their method works.

2. *Nothing succeeds like success.*
   Like money in a savings account, success seems to compound itself. A person who has a small success expects it to be followed by a bigger one.

3. *The end justifies the means.*

   It does not matter how you succeed. Any method is all right if it works for you. This proverb is not always accepted. Often one hears the opposite, "The end doesn't justify the means."

4. *All's well that ends well.*

   Similar to previous proverb. If we can come to a successful conclusion, let us forget about the pain and mistakes along the way.

5. *Killing two birds with one stone.*

   A clever person may sometimes achieve two unrelated things with one action. For example, a person might go to a gym for regular workouts partly for the benefit of the exercise and partly because he wants a chance to talk to some of the other people who also go to that gym.

6. *All's fair in love and war.*

   Do not trust a rival or an enemy at all. His or her desire to succeed will overrule everything else. Such a person may lie, cheat, attack, or do many other things far more terrible than he or she would normally do.

7. *If you can't beat 'em, join 'em.*

   If you cannot compete successfully with a person or group, stop competing and go join them. Then you can share in their success.

8. *Always a day late and a dollar short.*

   A criticism of a person who never succeeds. The failures may not be drastic, but the pattern of small failures is annoying to others, especially in two areas that Americans value as highly as time and money.

The "American Dream" is a dream of individual success, and it has come true for many "self-made" people. They set their goals. Their hard work has paid off. The whole nation admires their achievements. This is especially true of highly successful people who came from ordinary or poor backgrounds, such as Henry Ford, Marilyn Monroe, Billy Graham, Oprah Winfrey, and Michael Jordan.

Success stories like these inspire us all to try to make a success of ourselves. We dream big dreams. Children all over America are pushing themselves to see if they can become the next Michael Jordan.

Ambition, self-confidence, and hard work are admired. A certain amount of toughness and aggressiveness will be needed. Cleverness is also important. The clever person can *kill two birds with one stone* (5) — that is, succeed in two ways through one action.

Sometimes success can be so important that people will do anything to achieve it. We may even try to cheat our competitors, or we may switch sides in a competition in order to be on the winning side. But the best success is one that we win "fair and square," overcoming all problems without using any bad methods.

Success such as winning the lottery may be envied, but it is not admired because it comes through luck rather than effort or cleverness. People who never succeed in doing anything right are looked down on. They are *always a day late and a dollar short* (8).

***If you are NOT an American,
ask an American . . .***

- Can you name two or three people you would consider very successful Americans? Why do Americans admire these people so much?

- What kinds of things do Americans have in mind when they talk about "being a success in life"?

- Have you ever killed two birds with one stone? How did you do it?

Setting goals and choosing strategies

9. *One thing at a time.*
   Concentration leads to success. The person who tries to do too many things at once may fail at all of them.

10. *When in Rome, do as the Romans do.*
    Flexibility leads to success in unfamiliar circumstances. People may change their normal way of doing things in order to fit in better with those they are visiting.

11. *Don't put the cart before the horse.*
    Do things in a sensible order. For example, do something to impress your boss before you ask for a raise in pay. Don't ask for the raise first.

12. *Easy does it.*
    Some things require gentleness for success. One should not push too hard. Force may cause damage.

13. *Flattery will get you nowhere.*

   If flattery (insincere praise) is recognized, it will not succeed. One sometimes hears the opposite, *Flattery will get you everywhere.*

Americans have been described as pragmatists, that is, people who do whatever works toward achieving their goals. This, of course, assumes that every person has goals and thinks about them. Most Americans do, both in their personal lives and at work. "Mission statements" (one-sentence summaries of an organizational goal) have become popular in American business. Even schools and hospitals write mission statements.

Once a goal is set, an appropriate strategy may be chosen. The proverbs describe many strategies — concentration, flexibility, common sense, and gentleness. The wise person knows which one will bring success in each situation.

The goal becomes the measure of success. If we achieve a goal, we celebrate. If we don't, we find another strategy.

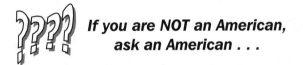 **If you are NOT an American, ask an American . . .**

- Americans seem to think a lot more about goals than we do in our country. What kinds of goals do you have for yourself this month or this year? Do you have goals for your whole life?

- Can you give me an example of a mission statement? Why would a hospital have to write a mission statement? Isn't it obvious what a hospital is supposed to do?

- Suppose I wanted to live by the saying "When in America, do as the Americans do." What should I learn to do in an American way? What will help me fit in? What will make me look like a foreigner who does not fit?

Confidence of Success

14. *Go for it.*
    Go ahead and try to achieve your goal. Don't worry about failing.

15. *Where there's a will, there's a way.*
    Any problem can be solved if one is determined enough.

16. *The sky is the limit.*
    Anything is possible. Prospects for success are excellent.

17. *So far so good.*
    Said by or to someone who is carrying out a plan taking one step at a time. Confidence increases with each step.

18. *We'll cross that bridge when we come to it.*
    Similar to previous proverb. We will not discuss or worry about a future problem. If and when the problem becomes urgent, we will deal with it.

19. *Practice makes perfect.*
    Effort brings improvement and success.

20. *The bigger they are, the harder they fall.*
    Do not be discouraged by the size of your problem or the fame of your competitor. (The saying is traced to a boxer preparing to fight an opponent much larger than he was.)

21. *Every little bit helps.*

   If someone apologizes for giving only a small gift, the recipient may encourage the giver by quoting this proverb. This is especially true if there is a huge job to do or a huge amount of money to be raised from many people.

As we push for success, we think that almost anything is possible. We encourage each other to take risks, to *go for it* (14). Perhaps this is because we are mostly people (or descendants of people) who left the land of our history and moved to America because it offered a better future for us and our children. That was a huge risk. For most Americans, that risk paid off. It seems to have increased our confidence. Today we are a nation of risk-takers — look how many of us have money in the stock market! We will return to this idea later in the section on optimism.

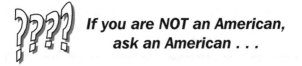

If you are NOT an American, ask an American . . .

- Americans seem to have a "can do" attitude toward life. You say, *Where there's a will, there's a way* (15). Do most Americans really think like that?

Taking risks cautiously

22. *Look before you leap.*

   Do not jump into a situation carelessly. You may land in difficulty.

23. *Curiosity killed the cat.*
   Similar to previous proverb. Do not ask too many questions or become too curious about things. You may get yourself into trouble, like a cat that does not see the danger in a new situation.

24. *All that glitters is not gold.*
   Do not be fooled by worthless things that seem valuable or look attractive. "Fool's gold" is the popular name for a kind of stone that glitters like gold but contains no gold at all.

25. *Too good to be true.*
   Similar to the previous proverb. This is often used to warn about advertising. An offer looks good but turns out to be misleading.

26. *There is no such thing as a free lunch.*
   Similar to the previous two proverbs. If someone you do not know offers you a free lunch or other gift, watch out. The gift may be a method of getting something from you.

27. *Seeing is believing.*
   This may be used as a polite way of saying, "I don't believe what you have told me. I'll have to see it for myself." Or it may be used by people who have just seen something that seems unbelievable.

28. *There is more here than meets the eye.*
   Be careful. People are hiding something in order to protect themselves or take advantage of you.

29. *Where there's smoke, there's fire.*
   Similar to previous proverb. Danger is about to flare up. For example, a person who talks about killing

herself may actually do it, as smoke may actually burst into flame.

30. *Time will tell.*
Wait and see how something will work out. Do not trust a person or thing too much right now. For example, a person may be asked if she believes her friend's apology. She may reply, *Time will tell*, that is, "I am not sure yet. As time goes by, we will see whether he acts like the apology was sincere or not."

31. *Better safe than sorry.*
It is better not to take a risk than to take a risk foolishly.

32. *Don't put all your eggs in one basket.*
Do not risk everything in one place or on one project. Divide your resources so that one failure will not ruin you.

33. *A bird in the hand is worth two in the bush.*
A thing you already have is worth twice as much as a thing you might get in the future.

34. *Don't count your chickens before they are hatched.*
Similar to previous proverb. Do not become too confident of success before you can see that progress is happening.

35. *Pride goes before a fall.*
Do not be overconfident and careless. Your circumstances may change quickly, and the emptiness of your bragging will be exposed.

36. *Don't bite off more than you can chew.*
Don't attempt something too large for you to handle.

37. *Hindsight is always 20/20.*

Looking back on the past, it is easy for anyone to see what should have been done even though it was impossible for anyone to see it at the time. ("20/20 vision" is an eye doctor's term for excellent vision. It refers to twenty feet, a standard distance for reading posters during an eye examination.)

38. *The burned child shuns fire.*

Some of life's lessons are learned the hard way. The person who has had to pay for a mistake will be careful not to make that mistake again.

39. *Once bitten, twice shy.*

Similar to previous proverb. This may also be used to explain the behavior of a person who is overly cautious about something. For example, if a person was injured in a traffic accident at a certain corner, he may always become nervous when approaching that corner. He may even avoid passing that corner at all.

Being great risk-takers, Americans have a lot of experience with things that go wrong. We therefore have many proverbs about danger. Most of these do not discourage risk-taking but rather give guidance about what to keep in mind while taking risks. Several have to do with seeing, such as, *Look before you leap* (22), *All that glitters is not gold* (24), *Seeing is believing* (27), and *There is more here than meets the eye* (28).

Some have to do with interpreting what is seen. One should not ignore evidence of a problem because *Where there's smoke, there's fire* (29). Something that looks good might be *too good to be true* (25). *Time will tell* (30).

Some sayings have to do with learning from looking back on life. *Hindsight is always 20/20* (37). Some of life's lessons are learned the hard way, that is, "in the School of Hard Knocks." One does not want to be a slow learner in that school. The wise person makes mistakes but does not usually make the same mistake twice. *The burned child shuns fire* (38). *Once bitten, twice shy* (39).

Risk-taking is usually admired but is still unwise if it is unnecessary. Do not be overconfident, thinking that every risk will succeed. *Better safe than sorry* (31). *Don't bite off more than you can chew* (36). *Pride goes before a fall* (35), not before a success.

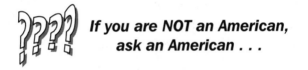

If you are NOT an American, ask an American . . .

- Can you give me an example of a situation where you might say each of the following things: *Look before you leap, There is no such thing as a free lunch, Hindsight is always 20/20.*

Facing setbacks with determination

40. *Nobody bats 1000.*

    No one succeeds all the time. Do not be discouraged by failures even if you have many of them. (The phrase comes from baseball, where a batting average is calculated for each player, using 1.000 to represent 100 percent. If a batter succeeded ["got a hit"] every time, his average would be 1.000, but in fact the best batters usually average only between .300 and .350.)

41. *When the going gets tough, the tough get going.*
    When the situation is difficult, the determined people can handle it. They do not give up.

42. *It isn't over till the fat lady sings.*
    I refuse to admit defeat yet. Though right now it looks like I may fail, there is still time for things to change. (The "fat lady" is an insulting reference to an opera soloist. Operas often end with a female solo.)

43. *While there is life, there is hope.*
    Do not give up even if you cannot see any way that your situation will improve.

44. *Rome wasn't built in a day.*
    Do not be discouraged if your goal still seems far away. On a big project, success takes time.

45. *If at first you don't succeed, try, try again.*
    Do not be surprised if your first attempt is not completely successful. Do not lose confidence in yourself. Don't give up.

46. *There are other fish in the sea.*
    Contrast to previous two proverbs. It is okay to abandon a goal sometimes. Look for other opportunities. For example, this may be used to encourage someone who has just broken off a relationship with a sweetheart.

As we saw in the previous section, Americans are confident that success is possible, or we would not attempt things. We are also sure that success is difficult. In fact, difficulty is what makes success so sweet to us. How could we be proud of our achievements if they were easy?

As we take risks, we expect difficulty. At first it may seem that a risk is not paying off, but if we do not give up, we may find success in the end. Perhaps we did not make our first attempt in the best way, but we could do better if we kept trying. Perhaps the task was too big or the time was not right. We need to be patient and determined. *When the going gets tough, the tough get going* (41).

Once in a while we have to admit that we cannot achieve a goal. In that case we choose a different goal, saying, *There are other fish in the sea* (46). We do not stop seeking success; we start looking for another way to succeed.

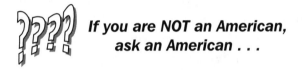

If you are NOT an American, ask an American . . .

- In my book there are a few comments about American baseball. Can you explain this to me? What is a batter? What does it mean that *Nobody bats 1000?*

- How closely do you agree with this proverb: *When the going gets tough, the tough get going?* Is that how you live your life?

 **DANGER**

If you ARE an American, watch out for cross-cultural trouble here

American readers may assume that focusing on success is a universal human trait, not an American cultural trait. Doesn't every human being want to be a success? Isn't success the most important thing in life in all cultures, even if it is defined differently?

The short answer is, "No." While some cultures such as the Chinese may be as pragmatic and success-oriented as American culture, they are the exception. Success implies several other things that are not central concerns in many cultures — setting goals, working hard for change, and using personal achievements as the basis for making judgments about a person's worth.

Some other cultures center their values on social harmony, defense of an ethnic/racial community, maintenance of the status quo, or transcendence of personal existence. An American may describe these as different ways of defining success, but people in other cultures will usually not look at their central value that way.

Disagreements about the importance of success can easily cause conflict. When we Americans press for success and change, some other cultures see us as insensitive, pushy, and disruptive. They do not welcome some of our changes. We may then regard them as thickheaded and lazy, unconcerned about improving their lives. Big mistake! Neither side realizes that the cultures simply disagree about whether life should center on individual success or not. Americans have a very hard time imagining that a worthwhile or intelligent life could focus on anything else.

Chapter Three

Self-Esteem and Fun

. . . .

Self-Esteem — The Dignity of the Individual

☑ 47. *Live and let live (Commandment 2).*[1]
Do not be judgmental. Do not try to control or punish other people. You live as you like and let others live as they like.

48. *To each his own.*
Each individual should be allowed to have his or her own preferences. People will naturally choose different activities, goals, religions, lifestyles, etc.

49. *Looking out for number one.*
Looking out for one's own personal welfare more than anything else. This is sometimes used to criticize a person who has abused or taken advantage of someone else: "All he was doing was looking out for number one." Or it may be used by a person to defend himself or herself: "There is nothing wrong with what I did. I was just looking out for number one."

---

1. See also *Celebrate diversity* (129).

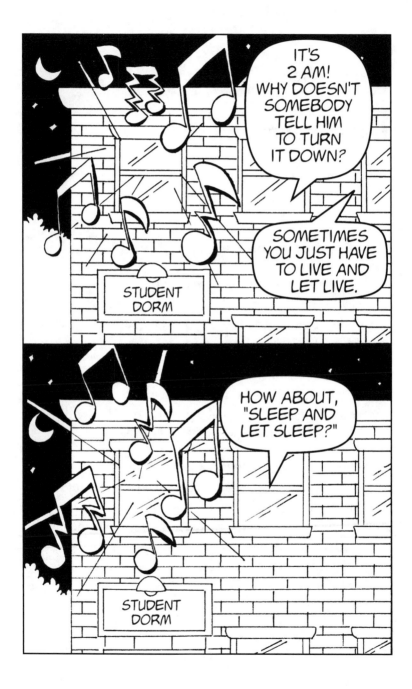

50. *Be true to yourself.*

Do not compromise yourself or your beliefs in order to please other people or fit in with a system. Know who you are. Let other people know what you stand for. Do not give in to pressure to conform or to do things you do not agree with.

51. *The customer is always right.*

Businesses instruct their clerks not to do anything that might threaten a customer's self-esteem, no matter how unreasonable the customer is. Any employee must carefully and politely hear any complaint of any customer. The customer must not be made to feel ignorant.

Though there are far more proverbs about success than self-esteem, the few proverbs about self-esteem are crucial to American thinking. The five proverbs quoted above are the foundation for the American understanding of everything that is normal, good, and right. All five are commonly used, and all five have wide implications.

Americans think it is natural and healthy for every person to be *looking out for number one* (49). From kindergarten onward, schools and parents tell children how "special" each one is. Even if children do poorly in their schoolwork, teachers avoid giving them low or failing grades because that may damage their self-esteem, that is, their sense of self-worth. They will feel like failures, not successes. The philosophy of life is, "Express yourself," "Enjoy yourself," "Respect yourself," *Be true to yourself* (50).

A best-selling book had the title, *I'm OK, You're OK.* For hundreds more books that will build your self-esteem, look in the self-help section of any American bookstore. American culture has adopted the view of the psychologist Maslow, who taught that "self-actualization" (fully becoming the person you could become) is the highest level of human development. Even the U.S. Army has accepted this view. It changed its recruitment slogan from a duty slogan, "Uncle Sam wants you!" to a self-development slogan, "Be all that you can be." ("Uncle Sam" is a mythical old man in a top hat and clothing that resembles the American flag. His initials, "U.S.," show that he is a symbol of the United States.)

Like a desire for success, self-esteem can be seen as a core value of American culture. Self-esteem, which is closely related to personal dignity, is often seen as the most basic human right and the key mark of a psychologically healthy person. Nobody wants to have low self-esteem, and nobody wants to associate with people who do.

Whatever promotes self-esteem is good, and whatever diminishes it is bad. That is why racism, sexual harassment, child abuse, male chauvinism, and religious intolerance are so unacceptable in America today. They all attempt to assert one person's dignity in a way that tears down the dignity of someone else.

We even have a new term for such things. We say they are not "politically correct." This may easily confuse foreigners for at least two reasons. First, "political correctness" has nothing to do with politics. It simply means what is "socially acceptable."

Second, it covers up a contradiction in our culture. Though we say, *Live and let live* (47) and we claim to be very tolerant, we absolutely do not tolerate attacks on self-esteem. In other words, though it is a terrible thing to condemn anyone for being "morally incorrect" or "theologically incorrect," it is a very good thing to condemn people for being "politically incorrect." This is true even though so-called political correctness is actually a matter of personal conduct (morality) and belief (theology). "Political correctness" defines what is not tolerable in a society that claims to tolerate anything.

Another thing foreigners may not immediately see is the connection between self-esteem and American informality. Regardless of age or rank, most of us Americans are called by our first name (except doctors, teachers, and military people). In many countries that would be interpreted as an insult to the older or higher-ranking person.

In America we see insults in the opposite way. We want to think we are all on the same level. Dignity and self-esteem have more to do with our humanness (the same for all of us) than with our rank (different for each of us). Anyone who insists on being called by a title rather than a first name is insulting the human dignity of all the lower-ranking people.

If you are NOT an American, ask an American . . .

- I am surprised to read that "self-esteem" is so important to Americans. I am not sure we even have a word for it in my language. Is it the same thing as personal dignity? How would you describe it?

- Can you tell me why your self-esteem is important to you? Is anything more important?

- Is *looking out for number one* always a good thing? Is that how most Americans live?

 **DANGER**

If you ARE an American,
watch out for cross-cultural trouble here

Most Americans consider self-esteem and fun to be universal human desires, just like success. But when a culture is not centered on success, then the basis for self-esteem and the importance of fun are also redefined. For example, in less individualistic cultures, self-esteem does not rest nearly so heavily on individual achievement. The important thing is one's relationship with the extended family, the village, or the clan. What the larger group thinks of me ("group-esteem") is far more important than what I think of myself ("self-esteem").

As some other languages have no word for "self-esteem," so the English language has no adequate word for this "group-esteem" (what the group you belong to thinks of you). "Reputation," "respect," or "regard" may be the closest terms, but none of them are as highly charged as the word "self-esteem." Imagine an American counselor probing a troubled person's mind to find out if something was wrong with her "group-esteem"! Now imagine how lost you could be in a culture where self-esteem meant nothing and group-esteem meant everything.

This is why people in other cultures spend so much time consulting everyone before they take action. They are making sure they don't damage their group-esteem. It is one of the most valuable things in life. To lose any esteem from the group would be such a disaster that they will not risk it.

When Americans do not consult others and therefore do risk such disasters, members of more group-oriented cultures take us to be arrogant and self-centered, despising and disregarding the importance of group-esteem. Ironically we are most likely to fall into this trap exactly at the time we are trying to impress local people with some amazing new initiative of ours. We impress them, all right, but not with the kind of impression we want to make.

Fun

52. *Time flies when you're having fun (Commandment 3).*
    A day seems short when it is full of enjoyable things but it seems like an eternity if one is idle or stuck with a boring job.

53. *If it feels good, do it.*
    Live according to your desires at the moment. Forget about rules, regulations, or consequences. Just have fun.

54. *You only go around once in life.*
    Enjoy life, do what you want to do, experience everything you can. A beer company expanded this proverb into an advertising slogan by adding, "so grab for all the gusto you can get." ("Gusto" is a slang word for zest, vitality, strength, fun, and enthusiasm.)

55. *All work and no play makes Jack a dull boy.*
    This is used to criticize someone who takes work too seriously. It affirms that play is an essential part of human life. ("Jack" is a very common name, used here to represent anyone.)

56. *Are we having fun yet?*

This is a sarcastic question. People who really are having fun do not have to ask such a thing. The question calls attention to the fact that something is not fun at all. For example, if someone reluctantly went along on a camping trip and it rained the whole first day, the person might ask this question to the group that had promised it would be a fun day.

57. *The more the merrier.*

This is a way of welcoming someone to participate. It means, "Of course you are welcome. The bigger the group, the better the party."

58. *It takes two to tango.*

Some desirable things are impossible for one person alone. They can be enjoyed only by two people who agree to cooperate very closely and move exactly together, as when dancing the tango.

Some people build their whole lives around fun. They say, *If it feels good, do it* (53). Though most Americans do not go quite that far, we do spend a lot of time looking for ways to have more fun.

Weekend time is fun time. Families have fun together. On vacations people go wherever they will have the most fun. Sex is fun. New experiences are fun. Hobbies are fun. The people we like are the ones who are "fun to be with." We even say, "She's a fun person." We wish that our whole lives were fun, and they would be (we think) if we did not have to spend so much time working.

Americans are so individualistic that it seems that golf and tennis would be more fun than other sports. For some strange reason, we love team sports in which everything depends upon each member of the group playing his or her role in constant and perfect harmony with other team members. This is particularly true of American football and basketball.

We seem to recognize that, like success, fun is even more enjoyable when it is shared with other people. That may happen with a sports team, at a party, or just with a good friend or lover.

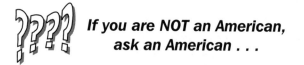

If you are NOT an American,
ask an American . . .

- What do you do for fun?
- Are you a fan of any professional sports team? Why do you like that sport and that team?
- Who are your favorite friends to have fun with? What do you do together? If I asked to come along sometime, would you say, *The more the merrier* or *Three is a crowd* (see proverb 146)?

 **DANGER**

If you ARE an American,
watch out for cross-cultural trouble here

Conflict about fun is much less common than conflict about many other cultural values and patterns. However, there is one major mistake that Americans make concerning fun when we are in another culture. Like typical foreigners, we spend most or all of our "fun" time with people of our own culture rather than with local people.

Having fun along with local people may seem too much like work, or it may depend too heavily on use of a local language. Local "fun" activities or celebrations may not look very enjoyable to us as outsiders. We may not get invited, and we may wonder whether we should look for a way to invite ourselves.

Nevertheless, it is worth a try. Having fun together can be one of the best bridges between cultures. Having fun apart from each other, each in our own cultural ways, can be one of the thickest insulators.

Conflicts among the Three Primary Goals

59. *You can't have your cake and eat it too.*

   Make up your mind. Sometimes one must choose between two very desirable things, giving up one in order to enjoy the other. If you have a piece of cake, you can save it to eat later. If you eat it now, you do not have it anymore.

Like all cultures, American culture has core values that do not fit together perfectly. Individual success, self-esteem, and fun may not be achievable at the same time. For example, success in a career may require such long working hours that the person has no time or energy left for fun. The term "workaholic" is used to criticize a person who never has fun because he or she is addicted to work just as an alcoholic is addicted to alcohol. On the other hand, if a student spends too much time having fun and too little doing schoolwork, he or she will not succeed in earning a college degree.

Success may also clash with self-esteem. Some Americans think that self-esteem is a birthright, like freedom of speech or freedom of religion. They do not believe that self-esteem should change, no matter how much one succeeds or fails. However, this position is very hard to maintain when individual success is so important.

Self-esteem and fun may also conflict with each other, especially when it comes to health and fitness. Many Americans complain that being overweight lowers their self-esteem. They go on diets regularly, but they also give up their diets regularly because dieting is not as much fun as eating. Exercising is not as much fun as watching TV.

The irony of the situation may be clearest at grocery store checkout counters. As Americans are in the very act of buying an entire shopping cart full of fattening junk food, we are faced with a whole rack of magazines with slender young women on the covers and articles about weight loss inside. Our solution is often to buy one of the magazines, and perhaps one or two of the candy bars which are always right next to them!

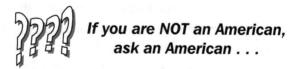

If you are NOT an American, ask an American . . .

- My book says that success, self-esteem, and fun are three of the most important things in American life. What do you think about that? How true is it for your friends?

- Do you know many workaholics? Do you pity them, admire them, or have some other attitude?

Just Three Goals but Thousands of Options

Success, self-esteem, and fun are common cultural goals, but each American gets to choose his or her own definition of these things. For example, swimming may be fun for one person but boring for another. Making lots of money may mean success to one person but not to another. When we consider our choices, we love to have lots of options. This is true in every aspect of life.

☑ 60. *Shop till you drop (Commandment 4).*
Shopping is a form of considering options. We think this is fun so we keep doing it until we are worn out. This saying is often used playfully, though it may take on more serious tones at Christmas — the only time of year when shopping seems to be a chore.

61. *Variety is the spice of life.*
Variety is what makes life pleasurable. Boredom is seen as a threat, and monotony is the surest route to boredom.

62. *There is more than one way to skin a cat.*
Any of several methods may bring about the desired result. Each person may choose the method that best suits her. If one method does not work, choose a different one and try again. (We Americans do not skin our pet cats. This saying goes back to the frontier days when "cat" also meant "wildcat." Wildcats were hunted for their valuable skins.)

63. *One man's meat is another man's poison.*[2]

Since the same thing may affect different people in different ways, each person must choose the things that will work in his or her particular case.

Though there may be no proverb (yet) which says so, American life seems to go by the principle, "More choices mean a better life." The saying *Variety is the spice of life* (61) comes close to it, but spice is merely something nice. Life does not depend on spice. By contrast, choice is the "bread and butter" (a basic necessity) of American life.

Multiplication of options and choices is evident everywhere in America. There are four hundred TV channels available on one satellite hook-up, hundreds of pictures and designs one can have imprinted on personal checks, dozens of flavors and types of dog food in the local grocery store, and a bewildering list of kinds of dressing you can order for your salad at a restaurant. Of course, no one can ever watch all the TV channels or use all the check designs. However, everyone seems to think life is somehow more successful or more fun because an individual choice was made from four hundred options instead of only three or four.

How do we American consumers keep up with all these options for a more enjoyable life? Advertising — TV and radio commercials, "junk mail," newspapers, telemarketers, Internet, billboards, T-shirts. We have a love-hate relationship with advertisers. On the one hand, they are invading our privacy and filling our minds with lots of information we do not want — I'll never buy a pickup truck, so why do I

---

2. See also *To each his own* (48).

have to watch fifteen truck commercials during every football game on TV? On the other hand, they are turning us into "smart shoppers," which we very much want to be, and of course they are talking about our highest values all the time — success, self-esteem, fun — so we find it hard to tune them out.

Our desire for more choices is one of the main reasons more and more of us live in urban and suburban areas rather than small towns or rural areas. One has more choices in a city. Never mind which choices they are or whether the small town had the exact choices you really wanted — the city must be better because it has more variety, more activity, more freedom of choice. If you want to be a success, to think highly of yourself and have lots of fun, go to the city.

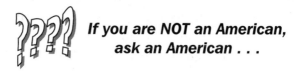

If you are NOT an American, ask an American . . .

- Why is it so important to Americans to have lots of options to choose from?

- If you were offered a job in a town of a thousand people, would you take it? Why or why not?

 ## DANGER

If you ARE an American, watch out for cross-cultural trouble here

We unconsciously make judgments about another city or country based on the number of channels on the TV set or the number of kinds of restaurants in town. If the number is low, we may conclude that we are in a second- or third-class country, a "hardship post," and resent it for the duration of our stay. Our smoldering resentment tends to come to the surface in critical comments. Then the local people naturally resent us. We resent them for resenting us, and things get worse.

It may not occur to us that a third-class consumer society could be a first-class society in other respects, and America could be a third-class society by other standards. For example, America is a third- or fourth-class society when it comes to maintaining quality relationships in the extended family. If you reply, "Surely having the mobility one needs for success is more important than living near all our aunts and uncles," you are simply expressing the American cultural point of view. It makes good sense within the American cultural framework, but it ought not be used to make judgments elsewhere.

Chapter Four . . . .

Ways to Achieve Three Goals at Once

. . . .

Of course, we Americans would like to enjoy success, self-esteem, and fun all at the same time with no conflict between them. We think we know at least three ways of achieving this — love, money, and playing to win. These are so important that some of us even value them for their own sake rather than as means to the three goals of success, self-esteem, and fun.

Love

64. *Love conquers all.*

Love overcomes all difficulties. For example, if a wife becomes crippled, the husband's love conquers that problem. He continues to care for her and be faithful to her.

65. *Love finds a way.*[1]

This is similar to the previous proverb. Love is considered one of the most powerful and determined forces in

---

1. See also *Where there's a will, there's a way* (15).

the world. Two people in love will "find a way" to get together.

66. *Love makes the world go 'round.*
    Love is the driving force in all of life. Love makes life worth living. If you understand love, you understand everything about life.

67. *Love is blind.*
    When people are in love, they do not see each other's faults.

68. *Absence makes the heart grow fonder.*
    When lovers are separated, they may think about each other constantly. Their love may deepen.

69. *Out of sight, out of mind.*
    Contrast to previous proverb. This is said of someone not considered important or worthy of loyalty. One forgets about that person as soon as he or she is out of sight.

70. *Marry in haste and repent at leisure.*
    Do not rush into any long-term commitment. In the past this meant, "Take your time before you commit yourself to a marriage partner." Now it often means, "Do not commit yourself to anyone. You will be sorry," or it may mean, "Live with a person for a while before marrying him or her." It may also apply to any long-term partnership, such as a joint business venture.

Love and sex feature very largely in American culture because they represent an obvious way to achieve all three primary cultural goals at the same time — success, self-esteem, and fun. Most Americans still see it as a success to have a steady, enjoyable love relationship (with or without marriage). Some men even see it as a "success" whenever they persuade any woman to have sex with them. A person's self-esteem goes up when he or she is loved by someone desirable. And sex is fun, along with all the flirtations leading up to it (at least that is how it is in the movies).

The view that the most important thing in life is to "fall in love," "be in love," and enjoy sex is most obvious in American popular music. One could even look at the popular songs at least since the 1950s as one long debate about a single question — is it or is it not possible for individualism to be overcome between two people through love? Many songs insist that *love conquers all* (64) and lasts forever. Many other songs deal with betrayal, pain, and recovery from loves that did not last forever.

One aspect of the debate is how sex and love are related, if at all. If sex is simply a playful experience between two consenting individuals, each meeting his or her own individual needs, obviously individualism is not overcome. But if two lives merge permanently on the sexual level as well as on many other levels in a love relationship, that is something altogether different. Americans in great numbers continue to show their faith in love by getting married. Even when they get divorced, it usually means they lost their faith in their marriage partners, not their faith in love. They keep looking for "true love" with a new partner, and many remarry.

The ideal of love is in direct conflict with the individualism of American culture. We wish the proverbs about love were true more often than they are in our experience, yet we are reluctant to live up to them.

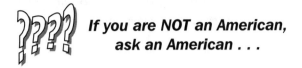

If you are NOT an American, ask an American . . .

- Do you think that people who are in a loving relationship with one other person have a higher self-esteem than people who are not in love? Why or why not?
- Lots of American songs talk about love lasting forever, but lots of other songs talk about broken hearts and lost loves. Which view is right? When people fall in love, do they stop *looking out for number one* or not?

 **DANGER**

If you ARE an American, watch out for cross-cultural trouble here

The contradiction between the glorification of love and the glorification of individual freedom may be the deepest contradiction in American culture. The myth and the pledge of eternal love are consistently defeated by the desire for individual freedom. This is obvious in the marriages (and affairs and divorces) of Hollywood movie stars, whose behavior is more and more typical of Americans from Little Rock or Walla Walla. Love does not conquer all, no matter what the proverb says.

If we have such difficulty figuring out how to keep two Americans in a lifetime relationship of love, what are the chances of an American making a cross-cultural love relationship work? It can be done (with delightful results), but it requires an unusual American or a very Americanized spouse.

Unfortunately *love is blind*, and lovers often underestimate the challenge of intercultural marriage.

Money

71. *If you're so smart, why ain't you rich?*
    This question implies that intelligence, like time, can be converted into money. It is used to cut down an ordinary person (not a rich one) who has expressed an opinion as if it is the final word on a subject.

72. *Money talks.*
    Wealth has influence. People who make big contributions to political candidates are "talking" to the candidates and expecting them to listen.

73. *Beggars can't be choosers.*
    Beggars have to accept whatever they get. A poor person has very few choices in life. This harsh reply may be used if people complain about the size or quality of a gift.

74. *Money can't buy happiness* (variant: *There are some things money just can't buy*).
    This reminds people that money is not an ultimate value although it often is treated as one. The saying may be used as a comment when a wealthy but lonely and wretched person commits suicide.

75. *Money isn't everything.*
    Same as previous proverb.

76. *The love of money is the root of all evil.*
    Greed will lead a person into many other evils, such as cheating, oppression, and violence. (One also hears

Money is the root of all evil, which places the blame more on money than on greed.)

77. *A fool and his money are soon parted.*
Folly will always show up in the way a fool handles money. Wise people are the ones smart enough to guard money once they have it.

Americans speak of "the almighty dollar" as if money were God. For many Americans it is God. Some of us worship it, we make any sacrifice to get it, we hold it dearly and protect it zealously. The acquisition of money is the center of life. It affects our choice of careers and almost everything else.

Several proverbs remind us that *Money isn't everything* (75). We know this, but we often do not act like we know it. Foreigners may take this as a sign that American culture is in serious trouble, and many Americans will agree.

Money is sometimes valued for its own sake but more often as both a symbol and a means to an end. Money is a symbol of individual success (unless one has inherited it). Wealth means one has taken initiative. Poverty means one has made no effort. Money shows that one has succeeded in providing for family members. Money also enables a person to buy other symbols of success, such as a fancy car and a big house.

Money is the means of increasing personal pleasure and freedom by increasing the number of choices open to a person. Wealthy people can vacation in Paris or Acapulco every year; the poor never get out of their own city or state. The wealthy can live in any neighborhood they want to; the rest have to live in whatever neighborhood they can afford.

If *a fool and his money are soon parted* (77), what can we say about the credit card? It is a method of parting people from their money before they even have it! A nation of credit card buyers would be a nation of fools if we believed this proverb. We obviously do not take it very seriously.

Money, like love and sex, is so important to Americans because it relates so closely to the three key values of success, self-esteem, and fun. Money is a symbol of success. My self-esteem, as well as other people's view of me, will automatically go up if I have more money. Money buys the ticket to all kinds of fun. With money a person can reach all three main goals of American culture. Without it, one can hardly reach any of them.

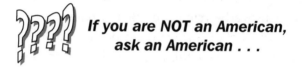

If you are NOT an American, ask an American . . .

- Americans work hard to get more money, but they complain that life is a "rat race" and everyone is too busy to enjoy it. Why don't more Americans take life a little easier and settle for less money?

- Suppose a good fairy offered you this choice — for the rest of your life you can have all the love you need or all the money you need. Which would you take and why?

 **DANGER**

If you ARE an American, watch out for cross-cultural trouble here

American cultural values focus on making money and holding on to it. Americans, especially those on "development" projects in other countries, are surprised that people in poor countries seem so uninterested in the latest American techniques for doing this. It is easy to conclude from an American perspective that the local people are lazy, stupid, or both, and that it is impossible to "help" them.

We do not see that their primary concern is often with spreading existing wealth around rather than making money or managing it. They ask two questions that Americans rarely consider: 1) how can I share the money I have in order to strengthen my relationships with the people who matter to me? and 2) how can I hold those people accountable to do the same kind of sharing for my benefit?

Their starting assumption about money is completely un-American. They believe that to accumulate individual wealth is antisocial. It insults the rest of the group, and it must be punished, not imitated. The right way to handle wealth is to share it by a very complex process of social osmosis (not a politically enforced communism) among all groups who are related to each other by family or clan.

The view of money that our proverbs promote is the view that many other cultures despise. They see Americans as antisocial on a global scale, not sharing our wealth even among ourselves. Instead we seem to suck the wealth from them and put it into secret vaults in the USA. Our international businesses and even our "aid" and "development projects" often come across as ways of teaching our money-sucking techniques to any local people who want to betray their own cultural values and become personally wealthy.

Playing to Win

78. *We're number one.*

    This phrase means, "We are the best." It is often chanted by the supporters of a sports team that has won a championship.

79. *It isn't whether you win or lose, it's how you play the game.*

    Playing well and fairly is more important than succeeding. This saying is sometimes used to console someone who has lost a game. The idea is that in spite of losing, one may still feel like a success if one has played as well as possible.

80. *Winning isn't everything.*

    One may enjoy the process of playing a game whether one wins or not. This traditional proverb is now often heard in the opposite form, *Winning isn't everything. It's the only thing.*

81. *Nice guys finish last.*

    Success is valued more highly than kindness and politeness. If unkindness and impoliteness contribute to one's success, they are sometimes excused as "toughness" or "what it takes." This is more often applied to men than women.

82. *The one who dies with the most toys wins.*

    This recent, cynical saying makes fun of three common American desires — competing, accumulating property, and having fun.

American play tends to be achievement-oriented and competitive. For example, in Europe when people go hiking, most do it primarily to enjoy the walk or the hike. Though Americans rarely turn a hike into an actual competition against fellow hikers, we do want to conquer something. As we hike we compete against the mountain, the weather, the clock, or our own aging bodies. We may enjoy nature a little bit along the way, but we are on the hike in order to prove we are capable of some praiseworthy feat.

What we are doing is trying to have fun and be a success at the same time. Play is not much fun if we fail to hike to the top of the mountain or if we lose the game. Play is supposed to be enjoyable and reduce our stress, but if we fail as we play, we may become more miserable and suffer more stress.

We Americans want to "have it all." We do not like to give up one thing in order to gain something else. We want to have more money, but we also want to spend more money so that we have more things. We want to enjoy love that keeps getting better. We want the newest, the biggest, and the best. We want more of everything, including more free time in our schedules. We really do want to *have our cake and eat it too* (59).

That is one of the reasons we love the Internet. We have to. It is such an American thing. After all, it is instant, it is new, it is free (or almost free, by comparison with costs in many countries), it is fun, it is highly individualistic, it is private (in the sense that our friends or family usually do not know what we are doing on it), it multiplies choices by the million, it lets us shop from home, and it does not threaten our self-esteem (in a "chat room" we can pretend to be anyone we want to be). What more could an American ask for?

If you are NOT an American, ask an American . . .

- What is a "good loser"? Should I try to be one?
- How much time do you spend on the Internet each week? Does your use of the Internet make you feel more like a winner or a loser most of the time?

 ## DANGER

If you ARE an American, watch out for cross-cultural trouble here

"We're number one!" summarizes the American attitude toward the world. We have the biggest economy, the most influential music and movies, the most people immigrating legally or otherwise, the most powerful military force. We know this and so does everyone else, but they are not as happy about it as we are.

It does not help matters that we constantly want to be number one by a bigger margin. If this is the game of life, the rest of the world is sure we are guilty of unsportsmanlike conduct, trying to run up the score on a defeated opponent. Too easily we forget, *It isn't whether you win or lose, it's how you play the game.*

Chapter Five

Essentials for Achieving Any Goal

....

Americans assume two things about achieving any of our goals in life. First, each person must be free to pursue success. The purpose of government is to guarantee this freedom. Education and business are not supposed to create any barriers to this freedom. Second, each person must take initiative to use that freedom. In other words, government, business, and education give us opportunities, but we have to make successes of ourselves.

Freedom — Equal Opportunity for All

83. *Life, liberty, and the pursuit of happiness.*
These three "inalienable rights" of human beings were mentioned in the American Declaration of Independence in 1776. Liberty is the freedom to choose and to engage freely in all activities that relate to the process of choice making, such as public speech, public assembly, and worship. Citizens choose their government and its officers.

84. *The land of the free and the home of the brave.*
This concluding line from the national anthem reminds Americans of freedom as our hallmark and bravery

in war as the price of that freedom. The anthem was written after a battle in the War of 1812, when America defeated a British attempt to reestablish imperial control.

85. *We shall overcome.*
This phrase is the title of a song that became a theme for African Americans during the civil rights movement of the 1960s. It referred to overcoming discrimination and winning genuine freedom for minorities in America.

The "American Dream" of individual success depends on freedom for each and every citizen. When African Americans, women, and other groups object to discrimination in education, housing, or employment (both pay and promotions), they are saying our society is hypocritical, and they are often right.

We claim that the door to success is open to everyone, but actually the door is sometimes open wider for some people than others. We claim that "all men are created equal," but we often treat minorities as "second-class citizens."

The civil rights movement and more recently the feminist movement have successfully made their point in many places. Laws, policies, and personal behavior have changed because people recognized that America was not living up to its boast of being a "free country."

People with physical disabilities have also benefited from recent changes like special parking places for the disabled (who are identified by a special license plate on their vehicles), ramps for wheelchair access to public buildings, elevators required in all buildings with more than one floor, etc.

It is very important to understand that these protest movements were not challenging the core values of American culture. On the contrary, they were affirming them. Protesters were demanding freedom to make successes of themselves. They were protesting a system in which their hard work was not rewarded fairly. When the African American leader Martin Luther King made his famous speech "I Have a Dream," he was calling America to live up to its own values, not to adopt African ones.

Preserving American freedom is the only serious concern most Americans have about international affairs. For the past generation the communist world, particularly the Soviet Union, was seen as the great threat to American freedom. Since 9/11 we talk of the terrorist threat, but most Americans now have very little interest in international affairs.

You may be surprised to find out how little your American friends know or care about the politics or even the geography of the rest of the world. We do think people everywhere should enjoy "freedom" as we do, and we assume that dictators and communist governments are hated by most of the people they rule. However, we are far more interested in protecting our own freedom than in promoting freedom for other people.

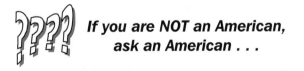

If you are NOT an American, ask an American . . .

- Do you think women and minorities are just as free as anyone else to succeed in America today? Can you give me some examples that have influenced your thinking?

- Where were you when you heard the news of the attacks on the World Trade Center? Did you feel like your own freedom was being attacked?

 **DANGER**

If you ARE an American, watch out for cross-cultural trouble here

If we live our whole lives in America, it is easy to believe the myth that at a global level our nation is nothing but the champion of human freedom and dignity. Everyone should like us and respect us for that. Everyone should adopt our values.

People in other countries are much more likely than we are to know of our blunders and even our hypocrisy in foreign policy over the years. For example, the human freedom we say we stand for has been trampled for over twenty years in southern Sudan (over two million deaths) and we barely notice, but as soon as Sudan is implicated as a country that may be harboring terrorists, we go into action. We spent almost nothing to stop the Rwanda genocide, but in Kuwait we spent billions to repel an invasion.

It is uncomfortable for us to hear from international acquaintances who believe that in their part of the world America has acted more like an enemy of freedom than a friend. We may not agree with their opinions, but we ought to hear them out concerning their facts. That could be good for everyone.

Personal Initiative

Freedom is like a sports field. It has to be cleared of other obstacles and activities so that people can play on it. But freedom can remain unused, just as a sports field can. By itself, freedom does not make anyone a success. Many American proverbs encourage people to take some initiative and use their freedom. In fact, there are so many proverbs about initiative that we have to break them into groups to deal with them.

Doing something is better than doing nothing.

86. *Just do it (Commandment 5).*
    This proverb is actually a recently invented advertising slogan for the Nike shoe company. It may also be the best three-word summary of American cultural values. It means, "Quit being indecisive. Don't bother consulting a lot of people. Don't waste much time on planning. Just do it and do it now. It will be okay. If not, you can always fix it later, or leave it for someone else to deal with."

87. *Talk is cheap.*
    Talking is not doing. It is easy to talk about a plan, but this gets little respect until one takes a risk and puts the plan into action.

88. *Put your money where your mouth is.*
    Similar to previous proverb. Get serious about what you are saying. When you have spoken in favor of something, prove that you mean it by betting on it or investing some money in it.

89. *Actions speak louder than words.*
Similar to previous two proverbs. To know people's hearts, pay more attention to what they do than what they say.

90. *The best defense is a good offense.*
Be proactive and goal-oriented, not timid or conservative. Aim to conquer, not merely to protect yourself.

91. *Never put off till tomorrow what you can do today.*[1]
Doing is better than waiting. If you wait, you might lose your opportunity.

92. *The road to hell is paved with good intentions.*
Like talking, intending is not doing. Actions matter far more than intentions. Actions determine where a person ends up.

93. *Idle hands are the devil's workshop.*
When people have nothing constructive to do, they get into mischief. The child who is bored may pick up a crayon and color on the wall, something that would not happen if the child were happily occupied in some other activity.

Americans are doers, and that means we achieve a lot in life. We do not accept bad situations as inevitable. We try to do something about them. We protest. We invent. We improve. We believe progress is possible and any individual can make it. We work hard without giving up, and we often succeed.

We assume that since our goals are noble and our intentions are good, people in all cultures will welcome our efforts to

---

1. See also *Opportunity only knocks once* (201).

improve things (such as the welfare of the average person in Afghanistan or Iraq). That is why we *Just do it* (86) when we have an idea. Later we may discover that we are on the road to hell even though our actions were based on good intentions (92).

Whether it is a huge movement as in Iraq or an individual American working on a development project in Tanzania or India, Americans get a reputation for being impatient and inconsiderate. We do not consult the people who should be consulted before action is taken. We ask directly for whatever we want. We think our American national symbol is an eagle, but the rest of the world thinks it should be a bull, the proverbial bull in a china shop.

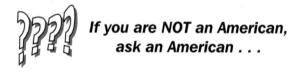

If you are NOT an American, ask an American . . .

- When have you used the saying *Just do it*, or when have you heard someone else use it?

Depending on yourself and your own actions

94. *Stand on your own two feet.*
    Grow up; act like an adult. Don't ask me to do something for you. This may be said to a young or immature person who depends too much on others. It is like a cow kicking a grown calf that still wants to suckle.

95. *If you want something done right, do it yourself.*
    This discourages people from trusting anyone except themselves. It may be said to someone who asks another

person to do a job for him or her and then complains about how it was done.

96. *You've got to take the bull by the horns.*
Grab directly and fearlessly for the toughest part of a problem. Do not look for an easy way out.

97. *Money doesn't grow on trees.*
You have to work for things. Success does not come on its own.

98. *Necessity is the mother of invention.*
When a person really needs something, he or she figures out some new way to get it. This creative initiative to change one's situation is considered much better than giving up and accepting things as they are.

99. *Too many cooks spoil the broth.*
Individual action or action by the smallest group possible is better than consulting a lot of people. Too much consultation will waste time and create problems. ("Broth" is the liquid in soup.)

100. *Easy come, easy go.*
If you have received something without working for it, it may soon be gone. You will not be as careful with it as you will be with something you earned.

In America, growing up means becoming independent, *standing on your own two feet* (94). Children are dependent on others. Adults are seen as independent and self-sufficient. This contrasts sharply with many traditional cultures where growing up means becoming interdependent with other adults. In those cultures the main questions in life are, "Whom can I depend on?" and "Who can depend on me?" Americans do not take those questions very seriously. We just assume it is safer to depend on ourselves.

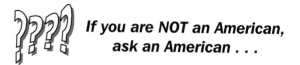

If you are NOT an American, ask an American . . .

- You say, *If you want something done right, do it yourself.* In our country we would rather say, "If you want something done right, get some friends to help you." Doesn't our way make more sense than the American way?

Expecting approval for taking initiative

101. *No pain no gain.*
    One must put forth an effort in order to succeed. (This saying comes from physical fitness instructors. They say that if you do not exercise hard enough to make your muscles hurt, the exercise is not doing you much good.)

102. *There is no harm in trying.*
    A person expects to be respected for making an effort even if it does not succeed. This view encourages people to take risks.

103. *Nothing ventured, nothing gained.*
    Similar to previous proverb.

104. *First come, first served.*
    This saying is used when there is a limited supply of something such as tickets to an event or food at a picnic. The idea is that no matter what your status, if you want

some of what is being given away or sold, you must present yourself in person and in good time.

Americans believe success is better than failure, but failure is better than not trying. When we fail we say, "At least I tried." We expect people to respect us for trying. We think they will forgive us easily if we tried in a wrong way as long as our intentions were good.

We also believe that it is not impolite to rush to get to the front of a line in order to try to get something before it is all gone. Many things in American life work on the basis of the saying *First come, first served* (104). The people at the front of the line are not insulting the people behind them. They just took more initiative or took it sooner. This is more likely to be admired than criticized by the people who came later.

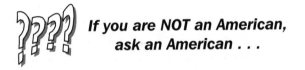

If you are NOT an American, ask an American . . .

- In my country it is a great disgrace to fail, so we do not try things unless we are fairly sure we can succeed. But in America, you seem to try anything. Do you really think it is better to fail at something than not to try it?

Knowing the proper limits of initiative

In most cases Americans like initiative but not always. Some proverbs warn us about initiative of certain kinds.

105. *Give him an inch and he'll take a mile.*
     Be careful of presumptuous people who take more initiative than they should. If you do someone a small favor

or delegate a little permission or a little power, he or she may take advantage of you.

106. *Fools rush in where angels fear to tread.*
Fools take initiative when they should not. They carelessly blunder into danger. Angels, considered to be powerful beings, are also wise enough to be cautious.

107. *If it ain't broke, don't fix it.*[2]
Do not bother trying to improve something if it is already working satisfactorily. That is a waste of time, and you run the risk of breaking the thing while you are trying to improve it.

108. *Leave well enough alone.*
Similar to previous proverb.

109. *The cure is worse than the disease.*
Similar to previous two proverbs. While trying to solve one problem, we create an even bigger problem. We would have been better off if we had done nothing.

110. *Count to ten before you lose your temper.*
Do not instantly let your feelings control your actions. Slow down. Think before you react.

111. *All things come to him who waits.*
Sometimes patience is better than initiative.

These sayings caution us not to think that initiative is always good. Sometimes it is better to leave things alone than to try to improve them. Sometimes humility and patience may be the best route to success. However, we see these warnings as

---

2. See also *Let a sleeping dog lie* (182).

exceptions. In most cases we would rather take charge and try to make things happen as we want.

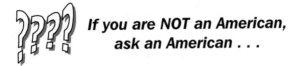

If you are NOT an American, ask an American . . .

- I don't understand how Americans decide when to take initiative and when to leave things alone. You say, *There is no harm in trying*, but you also say, *All things come to him who waits.* Can you explain this for me?

 **DANGER**

If you ARE an American, watch out for cross-cultural trouble here

Just do it is about the worst rule of thumb an American can live by in many other cultures. The way to get something done there is to consult your supervisor, your colleagues, the barber, the little old lady down the street, and a few other people first. If you get their blessing for your idea, wait a little longer. Then tentatively do about half of what you thought they said was okay. Believe it or not, you may still be considered pushy and out of line, but probably by a tolerable amount.

On the other hand, if you *Just do it* (86) without consulting, you are breaking all the rules. Local people will make you pay. You did not listen to them, so they will not listen to you. Any innovation you are trying to launch will die right before your eyes.

When Americans with good intentions see our innovations being killed, we often conclude that local people are against change. What the local people really are against is social insults. They will reject a proposed change, no matter how "beneficial," if it is introduced by bypassing the normal pattern of consulting relationships. The merits of an idea do not matter as much to them as the way the idea is introduced.

Chapter Six

The American View of Human Beings

....

Human Nature

112. *Nobody is perfect.*
Everyone has shortcomings. This is used as an excuse for a minor mistake that has been made.

113. *To err is human.*
Same as previous proverb. ("Err" means to make a mistake.) This saying is sometimes extended with the phrase, *To forgive is divine*, that is, it is normal for humans to make mistakes and it is godly (or God-like) to forgive them.

114. *There's many a slip between the cup and the lip.*
This refers to a plan that has gone wrong. When one is drinking from a cup, one intends to get all the drink into the mouth, but this does not always happen. The plan is good, but it can still fail.

115. *Boys will be boys.*
People will act according to their nature, including some mischief. This is sometimes used to describe irrespon-

sible but not too seriously wrong behavior by men. In other words, grown men will sometimes act like little boys.

116. *When the cat's away, the mice will play.*
People will take advantage of a situation if they can. Employees will get lazy if the supervisor is not keeping an eye on them. A teenage son or daughter might hold a wild party at home during a weekend when the parents have gone out of town.

117. *Better the devil you know than the devil you don't.*
People are generally not trustworthy. It is therefore better to deal with a familiar person or situation than an unknown one. That way you know what to watch out for, and you can protect yourself better.

118. *One bad apple can spoil the whole barrel.*
Do not associate with bad people. They may spoil you as a rotting apple spoils the apples next to it in the barrel.

119. *The grass is always greener on the other side of the fence.*
People are never satisfied with what they have. They always want what someone else has.

120. *Keeping up with the Joneses.*
This means buying things that you see your neighbors buying. That way you look like just as much a success as they do. (Jones is a very common name. "The Joneses" means "the neighbors.")

Americans recognize that all human beings have faults. *Nobody is perfect* (112), or as we saw in the earlier section on setbacks, *Nobody bats 1000* (40). We can keep a healthy self-esteem without thinking we are perfect. But we could not keep it if we thought we were basically evil.

This is how we convince ourselves that we are not evil. We claim there is no evil in watching out for our own good, (*Looking out for number one*, 49), or in saying, "That's just the way I am." We call this "self-preservation" and "self-expression." We see nothing evil about either one.

We define evil as the intent to harm. An evil person plans to harm others and enjoys doing it. If our self-preservation or self-expression harms someone even though we did not intend it, that is not evil. That's life. We may or may not feel bad about it. We may or may not do anything to make up for the damage. But we do not lower our self-esteem, and we do not see such accidental damage as evil.

There is a paradox in American culture at this point. Americans consider selfishness to be very bad, but self-interest (including self-esteem, self-sufficiency, self-preservation, and self-expression) to be very good. However, selfishness and self-interest are almost the same thing. How do Americans maintain a distinction between the two?

It is a very interesting question to discuss with Americans, most of whom have never thought about it. We may say something like, "A selfish person does not care about other people at all; a person with a healthy self-interest takes other people into account before acting." Or we may say that self-interest is a kind of "enlightened selfishness." Though we may not convince you, most of us will still insist that self-interest and selfishness are not at all the same.

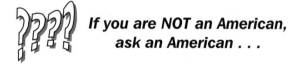

If you are NOT an American, ask an American . . .

- Americans seem to see a big difference between selfishness and self-interest, but aren't those two things very similar? What do you think the difference is?

- Would you agree that most Americans are basically focused on themselves but not basically evil?

DANGER

If you ARE an American, watch out for cross-cultural trouble here

One of the most basic and dangerous differences between cultures is what they will excuse and why. Americans living in other cultures tend to excuse themselves for behavior that the local culture considers inexcusable.

Self-expression, viewed as a fundamental human right by Americans, can get us into all kinds of trouble. "That's the way I am" can easily bring the response, "That's not the way we do things here." More often it can cause local people to withdraw from us, saying nothing at all.

We get ourselves into these predicaments because we are used to excusing our actions if we did not intend any harm. In another culture we have to learn to judge our actions by the amount of harm they inflict, intended or not. This simple but radical shift can pay great dividends to the Americans who are willing to make it.

Age

✓ 121. *You are only young once (Commandment 6).*[1]
      Do what you can while you are young. For example,
      go to Europe for a couple months during your sum-
      mer break from college. Once you graduate from college
      and begin your adult working life, that opportunity will
      be gone.

122. *A man is only as old as he feels.*
      A person's energy level is more important than age.

123. *Oh, for the vigor of youth again.*
      An expression used sadly by a middle-aged or older
      person, often when observing a child or youth doing
      something very active.

It has been said that most cultures worship their elders, but
America worships its children. Children represent possibilities, and we Americans love possibilities. A current national
campaign to reduce child abuse and promote volunteer men-
toring is called "Children First." Because of freedom of speech
in America, you may criticize almost anything. You may even
get away with criticizing a person's mother or father, but do
not make the mistake of criticizing someone's child.

Aging is seen only as a loss of liveliness and strength, not
an increase in prestige or wisdom. Everyone wants to "stay
young." Though the glory of the world lies in the future, the
glory years of any individual's life are thought to be in youth.
Middle age and old age are a battle to cling to the vitality and
freedom of youth for as long as possible. Cosmetic surgeons

---

1. See also *You only go around once in life* (54) and *You can't teach an old dog
new tricks* (217).

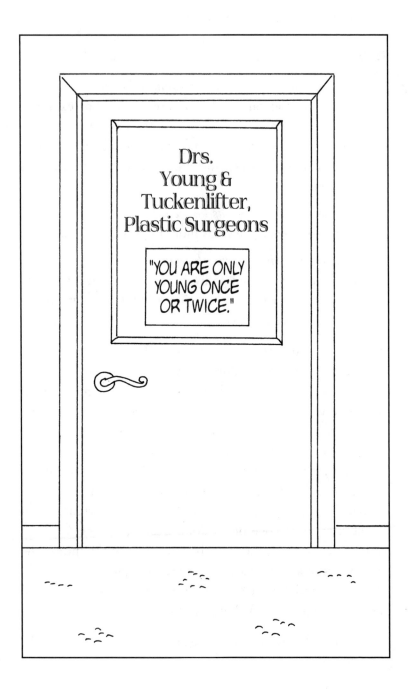

make a very good living because so many Americans want to hide the visible signs of aging.

Americans also love experiences, which may be the reason we see youth as the ideal time of life. It is a time of the most freedom, the most choices, the most vitality, all of which are highly valued. It is also the time of the fewest obligations, that is, the fewest limits to choices.

Retirement, usually beginning at age sixty-five, is seen as a time of self-indulgence. Many retirees move south because the weather is warmer. They may settle in a retirement community in Florida or Arizona, even though this means moving far away from relatives and friends. They take up a hobby or two or three. They fish, golf, read, shop, play cards, and travel. There is time to relax and enjoy whatever one can afford.

Retirement generally moves the retired people figuratively as well as geographically. It is as if they go off into a world of their own, fairly detached from the younger generations. Retired people do not expect to be looked up to or even paid much attention by younger people. They do not expect anyone to show special respect for them or seek their advice. Their children do not support them; they live on what they have saved and what the government provides through the Social Security program.

The flip side of the independence of retired people is that they have no obligations. They are "free" in a sort of ideal way. No one makes any demands on them. They may volunteer to help with some work of a community organization or church, but they will do only as much as they like.

People from other cultures may wonder whether retired Americans have any sense that they are worth anything as human beings. In most other cultures, that sense of worth would come from one's social interaction with younger people, especially relatives, and from the respect they show the elders. In America the sense of worth comes from looking at retirement itself as an achievement, perhaps the one great achievement to which the rest of life was looking forward. A retiree may say, "I worked all my life for it. I made money and saved money. Now I enjoy it." One of the most important differences between American culture and many others is that one's sense of worth comes more from personal achievements than from relationships. A great deal of American culture will not make sense to the outsider until this point is recognized.

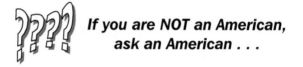 **If you are NOT an American, ask an American . . .**

- It seems that American families don't care about being far apart when the parents get old. Can you explain that to me? It's very different in our country.

- Do you see anything good about getting old?

- Do you agree that "one's sense of worth comes more from personal achievements than from relationships"?

Gender

124. *A man's home is his castle.*

At home a man is like a king, completely free to do as he wishes.

125. *A man may work from sun to sun, but woman's work is never done.*

Men may have to work long days but they can go home to rest in the evening. Women (working in the home or at an outside job or both) can never get away from what used to be called "women's work," such as cooking and cleaning.

126. *It's a woman's prerogative to change her mind.*

Since women are often considered more emotional and less logical than men, and since emotions are more changeable than reasons, women are allowed to change their minds. (A "prerogative" is a right. It is not something a person has to ask permission for.)

127. *Clothes make the man.*

The way a man dresses will affect the way he sees himself and the way other people see him. The implication is that if you want to succeed, dress for success.

128. *Beauty is only skin deep.*

Contrast to previous proverb. One should admire a person, particularly a woman, for her deep, inner character and not simply for her superficial beauty.

129. *Celebrate diversity.*

A recent slogan intended to promote acceptance of people different from oneself. It is often used by the homosexual community. In that case it means, "Do not criticize anyone because of his or her sexual orientation. Instead accept and even celebrate the fact that people have different likes and dislikes in sexual activity as in other aspects of life."

The definitions of male and female roles in American society are under fierce debate in America today. What makes a man masculine? What makes a woman feminine? Are men and women the same? How can a woman be fulfilled as a housewife if there is no obvious personal achievement and no pay? Is sexual orientation purely a matter of personal preference?

Because Americans are so divided about gender issues, most of the above proverbs about gender will offend somebody. For example, feminists are offended by sayings like *A man's home is his castle* (124), or *A woman's work is never done* (125). They believe these are old-fashioned, oppressive ideas. Similarly the saying *It is a woman's prerogative to change her mind* (126) may imply that women are less decisive than men and therefore inferior to men. A popular situation comedy in the 1950s had an old proverb as a title, *Father Knows Best*. Those would be fighting words in a lot of American homes today, where father and mother are supposed to be equal.

Traditionalists, who may not be bothered much by those proverbs, are deeply offended when homosexuals adopt the new slogan, *Celebrate diversity* (129). They do not believe that sexual orientation is a matter of free choice. Traditionalists consider homosexuality to be perversity, not just diversity, and they believe good citizens should not celebrate perversity.

The saying *Beauty is only skin deep* (128) is not offensive to many people, but we do not live by it anyway. It seems not to have much influence on American women or the men they seek to please. Compare the amount of time and money women spend on makeup with the amount they spend developing their inner beauty.

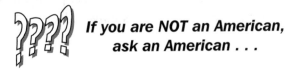

If you are NOT an American, ask an American . . .

- Do you agree with the slogan, *Celebrate diversity*? Why or why not?

- Do women have a different place in American society than they did ten or twenty years ago? What has changed and what else still needs to change (if anything)?

 **DANGER**

If you ARE an American, watch out for cross-cultural trouble here

Issues of age and gender present opposite problems for Americans living elsewhere. By comparison with our hosts, we tend to show less respect for the elderly but demand more respect for women. We consider respect for the elderly to be something that can vary from culture to culture, whereas respect for women is a universal requirement.

To other cultures, this sounds like we are saying, "Your cultural values, such as respect for the elderly, are okay within your culture but do not apply to us Americans. Our cultural values, such as respect for women, are universal human rights. If your cultural values go against these, then your culture has to change."

We may indeed want to insist that other cultures show more respect for women. It may be right to do so. But we have to realize that it is not persuasive simply to insist that other cultures accept our values as universal.

Chapter Seven

Loyalties, Groups, and Families

. . . .

Duties and Loyalties

130. *One good turn deserves another.*
     If you do something good for me, I should do something
     good for you.

131. *If you scratch my back, I'll scratch yours.*
     Same as previous proverb. (This refers to a pleasurable
     back-scratch, not an attack from behind.)

132. *A friend in need is a friend indeed.*
     My true friend is the one who shows loyalty to me by
     helping me when I am in need.

133. *A live dog is better than a dead lion.*
     It may be better to run away like a scared dog with
     its tail between its legs than to stand and fight to the
     death like a courageous lion. This can be used to justify
     cowardly behavior when a person has abandoned duty
     or loyalty in order to protect his or her own life.

134. *Rats desert a sinking ship.*
     A losing cause is abandoned. This is generally used to
     criticize the people who are abandoning a project, since
     they are compared to rats.

135. *A good captain goes down with his ship.*
     Contrast to previous proverb. The captain remains on
     board his ship even when all hope to save it is lost.

136. *My country, right or wrong.*
     Similar to previous proverb. I am absolutely loyal to
     my country whether or not I agree with its policy in a
     certain area.

137. *No man can serve two masters.*
     Divided loyalty will break down sooner or later.

138. *A dog is a man's best friend.*
     Dogs are known for their loyalty. Their friendship is
     more reliable than the friendship of people.

As we have seen in various other sections of this book, Americans' primary loyalty is to ourselves as individuals. *Be true to
yourself* (50) sums up this view. *Looking out for number one*
(49) is another way of saying it. All other duties and loyalties
have to be seen in light of this basic loyalty to self.

For example, loyalty to a cause may break down if the
cause seems lost. *Rats desert a sinking ship* (134). *A live dog
is better than a dead lion* (133). In both cases saving one's
own life is more important than the welfare of the cause or
the group.

Loyalty cannot be assumed on the basis of birth, custom,
or history. It must be earned continually. The person or group
desiring an individual's loyalty must keep on showing that the
individual will be better off by remaining loyal. For example,
a sports team that wants loyal fans must keep winning. The
political party that wants loyal voters must serve their interests. Even marriage partners may feel they have to keep

earning each other's loyalty, in spite of vows to stay together "for better, for worse."

An outsider may reasonably ask whether "loyalty" that has to be re-earned all the time is really loyalty at all. Is it anything more than a temporary association motivated by self-interest? This is a powerful and troubling question for American society. Loyalties to companies, to neighborhoods, and even to friends seem to mean less than they used to.

During the Vietnam War, a fierce debate about national loyalty began. Many Americans were motivated by the saying *My country, right or wrong* (136). They accepted military service, and many died in Vietnam because of this type of loyalty to their country. But there were also many war protesters who avoided ("dodged") the military draft. They did not consider themselves disloyal to America. On the contrary, they felt that the American government was being disloyal to the American people, and that the people loyal to America had to take drastic action to reassert their control over their own government. Eventually they forced a change in national policy. The scars of this bitter battle about national loyalty have still not completely healed after a generation.

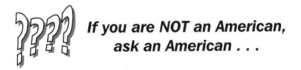

If you are NOT an American, ask an American . . .

- What loyalties do you have besides loyalty to yourself? How much have those loyalties been tested?

- Is there any person or group of people you expect to be loyal to you for your whole life, no matter what happens? Why will they be loyal?

 **DANGER**

If you ARE an American,
watch out for cross-cultural trouble here

Most Americans who live in other countries do not stay long enough to develop any loyalties there. The U.S. State Department deliberately keeps staff in one country only for short stays so they will not develop any loyalty there.

Whether we work for the government or not, we do not see this lack of local loyalties as a big problem since we come from a culture of transience. We function pretty well in America without the benefit of many loyalties.

In many other cultures, however, loyalties are essential for any significant things to be done. Loyalties evoke trust and build influence. Loyalties open doors. But loyalties take a long time to establish, and their price can be so high that we do not even consider investing in them.

In our haste we also tend to be oblivious to existing loyalties among local individuals and groups. Unless we pay attention to these, we will remain clueless in the loyalty department, causing serious miscalculations about our local relationships.

Groups

139. *Two heads are better than one.*
     Two people are more likely to succeed than one working or thinking alone. It is better to consult than to act alone.

140. *A house divided against itself cannot stand.*
Unity is the strength that preserves a family or a nation.

141. *Many hands make light work.*
Similar to previous proverb. Cooperation makes a job much easier.

142. *There is safety in numbers.*
Do not take large risks all by yourself. Do not walk alone on a dangerous street at night.

143. *Birds of a feather flock together.*
People with similar characteristics and interests will spend their time together. This may be used as a warning against associating with bad people. Others will assume one is like them.

144. *Blood is thicker than water.*
Blood relationship is stronger than voluntarily chosen friendship. Brothers will stick up for each other against their own friends if they have to. This proverb is not quoted much anymore because kinship is not as highly valued as it used to be.

145. *Misery loves company.*
When things go badly, a person wants a group of friends to share the pain. This can also mean that when people are miserable, they may want to make others miserable too. Such people are dangerous.

146. *Two is company and three is a crowd.*
Leave us alone. This may be used when two people are talking and a third, unwanted person approaches. The

implication is that the two people are comfortable together and they do not want someone else "crowding"
in on them.

One might suppose that Americans are so individualistic that
we have little use at all for belonging to any group. This is not
quite true. We have already seen that belonging to a group
can make fun more enjoyable and success more likely. For
example, *The more the merrier* (57), *Two heads are better
than one* (139), *Many hands make light work* (141).

Belonging to a group may also be important for other reasons such as safety (*There is safety in numbers*, 142), shared
interests (*Birds of a feather flock together*, 143), kinship
(*Blood is thicker than water*, 144), and a specific misfortune
(*Misery loves company*, 145).

Americans do not mind group relationships. What bothers
us is group obligations. We join groups easily and we leave
groups easily. In other words, we join groups that serve our
personal interests, and we remain with a group for as long as
we wish to enjoy it, but no longer. Americans' ease with group
relationships makes it easy for us to engage in conversation
or form casual friendships with complete strangers but very
hard for us to form deep and lasting relationships. Personal
freedom or self-development is rarely sacrificed for the sake
of a group.

Americans are skeptical of group loyalties because we associate them with tribalism, fundamentalism, and communism,
which we see as three main sources of conflict in the modern world. Rwandan-style massacres or Iranian-style Islam
occur only when tribal or religious loyalty is elevated above
"human rights" (that is, rights that each individual human

being has regardless of ethnic identity or religious belief). Soviet-style communism routinely put the good of the nation above the human rights of the individual citizen — an unforgivable sin in American eyes. Outsiders may rightly argue that Americans do not understand any of the three systems we criticize so strongly. However, all three seem to go against our proverbs.

Outsiders can see that our casual approach to groups leads to significant problems. American individualism can make us lonely, rootless, and empty. Growing problems such as family breakdowns and stress-related illnesses show that this really is happening. But we Americans still cling to our individualism.

Instead of thinking we are lonely, we just think we are bored. To break the boredom, we seek some new, exciting experience. We do not work on building relationships with a group. Perhaps one day we will decide the price of our individualism is too high, but we have not decided that yet.

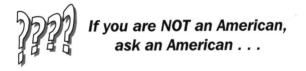 **If you are NOT an American, ask an American . . .**

- Do you agree that "Americans enjoy groups but don't like group obligations"? What do you think that says about Americans?

- What groups do you belong to that are an important part of your life? How long have you belonged to them?

 **DANGER**

If you ARE an American,
watch out for cross-cultural trouble here

American life patterns are subconsciously designed to maintain our personal space, while many other cultural patterns
are subconsciously designed to form groups. This puts
Americans out of sync with many other societies at a deep
level.

Local people trespass across our unconscious boundaries
of personal space (time, distance, or privacy). We pull back
and reinforce those boundaries that we just can't seem to live
without. The people we hold at a distance wonder why we
don't like them, and we wonder why they wonder that.

Since so few Americans take any initiative toward joining
any local group, those who do will be noticed. Often they
are warmly welcomed by local people who may have been
watching Americans from a distance for years.

The Family as a Group

147. *Charity begins at home.*
     One should be kind to close relatives before doing good
     to the community in general.

148. *Home, sweet home.*
     Often used on plaques hung on the wall, this phrase
     reminds people of the ideal home. It should be a place
     of warmth, love, and joy. The phrase may be used by
     people returning home at the end of a long trip.

149. *There is no place like home.*
    Similar to previous proverb. Home is the best place in the world, the most relaxing and enjoyable place.

150. *Home is where the heart is.*
    Home is wherever one's loved ones are. The size or appearance of a house does not make it a home or keep it from being a home.

151. *Baseball, motherhood, and apple pie.*
    Three things that all Americans supposedly like. Baseball was long considered the national sport. Motherhood was a role that everyone praised. Apple pie was the most popular dessert.

152. *Like father, like son.*
    A son will be like his father. This may be quoted whenever the son has done something that reminds people of the father, whether it is good or bad.

153. *Spare the rod and spoil the child.*
    An undisciplined child will turn out to be a rotten person. This proverb is highly controversial today. Many parents think that any physical punishment of children is abusive, while many others think that without it, children grow up to be morally retarded (or to be more acceptable they might say "morally challenged"). We can get into an ugly debate on this point.

The very first point to recognize in a discussion of American families is that Americans apply the word "family" almost entirely to the "nuclear family," not to the "extended family" as in most other cultures. Many Americans live hundreds or thousands of miles from their nearest "extended family" relative. Contacts with aunts, uncles, and cousins are often lost.

For example, I have about thirty or thirty-five first cousins, but I have seen only about five of them more than once or twice in the last twenty-five years. Several I would no longer recognize if I saw them on the street because I have not seen them or their pictures since childhood, and four or five I cannot even name. This is no doubt shocking to some readers from other countries, especially since in our family there are no bitter feelings keeping any of us cousins apart. The separation may be partly due to my having lived out of the country for fourteen of the last twenty-five years, yet this is not unusual even for Americans who remain in the United States for their whole lives.

Because of all the moving, many Americans do not have any one city they really call "home." We do not have a family cemetery. We do not have property in a "home town" that we intend to go back to in our retirement. Such things which are vitally important in many cultures are fading away from American culture.

The proverbs about home reflect the era of my parents' childhood much more than the situation today. Americans have a nostalgic view of home and family. As with the proverbs about love, we wish that the proverbs about the home were truer in our experience. *Home, sweet home* (148) sounds like wishful thinking to a lot of us today. Things are different now. Home is not where the heart is. Home is where the television is (though again, we have no proverb that says so, and most Americans may laugh at that phrase).

Everything about American homes is moving toward greater individualism. Watching television is an extremely individualistic activity, and Americans watch so much of it that we have started calling ourselves "couch potatoes," that is, people who sit on the couch and watch TV all day, as inactive as potatoes. Many American homes have several TVs so family members can watch different programs at the same time.

The microwave oven has had a huge though unintended destructive effect on American families in the last twenty years. It individualizes the process of food preparation. Each person can now create his or her own hectic schedule without having to consider meal time. Even children can prepare food on their own. Many families do not eat together at all anymore.

American houses are being designed with smaller common spaces (living rooms, dining rooms) and larger individual spaces (bedrooms with space for computers, desks, etc.). The tendency is for people to become increasingly isolated from other members of the family even while living under the same roof.

If we want to recover strong family relationships, our proverbs will not help us much. With the exception of *Spare the rod and spoil the child* (153) — not widely accepted anymore — there are no common American proverbs specifically about being a good parent, husband, wife, or child, or about showing special respect to a person in any of these roles.

There is much talk in America about a recovery of "family values." A popular religious movement in the 1990s called "Promise Keepers" filled football stadiums nationwide for weekend all-male conferences. Men were urged to keep their promises to wives, children, and God. The problem with such a campaign is that "family values" put limits on individual choices and freedoms. Not all Americans want to pay that price in order to improve family relationships.

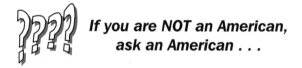

If you are NOT an American, ask an American . . .

- What does it mean when someone says, "America should get back to family values"? How far do you agree with that?

- How many cousins, aunts, and uncles do you have? When did you last see them?

 **DANGER**

If you ARE an American, watch out for cross-cultural trouble here

One of the most common and most fundamental mistakes of Americans in other cultural settings is to assume that the local person we are talking to is an individual. When we say, "How are you?" we mean "you" singular, not your whole family. In many languages the question is plural, "How are all of you?" That is the question we need to learn to ask.

Of course, family ties can be oppressive in some cultures. Favoritism to family members can corrupt whole countries when it is applied in the political arena. But we Americans have reacted against these dangers by going completely off the other end of the spectrum. In order to begin to understand people in other cultures, we need to remind ourselves that, for good or ill, family obligations and relationships mean vastly more to others than to us. Saying, "How is everybody?" or taking an interest in someone's parents or family tree can be a very instructive start.

Chapter Eight

Fairness, Blame, and Conflict

. . . .

Justice and Fairness

In any culture that places such a high value on individual success won by strategy, hard work, and wise risk-taking, one has to ask what is considered fair. Are there any moral limits to strategy? How does justice relate to success and to freedom?

154. *Enough is enough (Commandment 7).*
This very common proverb means, "I have had enough of the unjust things you are doing to me or to the ones I love. I am not going to take it anymore. I am going to act to put some justice into this situation." Americans highly respect people who stand up for their rights and change a bad or unjust situation.

155. *Silence is consent.*
Do not stay silent when you see a problem or an injustice. Speak out against it. Say, *Enough is enough* (154), or people will think you do not mind the situation.

156. *What goes around comes around.*[1]
What you do to others, especially if it is bad, will eventually be done to you. As you seek your own success,

---

1. See also *If you scratch my back, I'll scratch yours* (131).

do not treat other people badly. They may take revenge and spoil your success.

157. *Do unto others as you would have them do to you.*
Similar to previous proverb (which could be phrased, "Do not do to others what you do not want them to do back to you.") The "Do unto others..." form is the "Golden Rule" from the Bible. It is not a warning but a command — treat others justly.

158. *Turnabout is fair play.*[2]
If a person is taking advantage of someone else, the situation may change. The one on top may end up on the bottom. Then the one who has turned the tables will say, "Don't complain. I am only doing to you what you did to me."

159. *Two wrongs don't make a right.*
Contrast to previous proverb. If someone does a wrong to you, react with justice, not by doing something vicious. For example, if someone steals from you, do not steal from him or her. Have him arrested for stealing. He did wrong to you, but you do right in response.

160. *Honesty is the best policy.*
When one is tempted to cheat, this proverb serves as a reminder of the importance of good character. Honesty brings trust, and trust leads to success.

161. *Justice is blind.*
In a court of law, the judge must be blind to the status of the accused person. It should not matter whether the accused person is rich or poor, black or white, famous

---

2. See also *Don't get mad, get even* (189).

or unknown, a foreigner or a relative. This proverb is often symbolized by a picture of a blindfolded woman holding a pair of scales. She is thought to be weighing the evidence, not the people concerned.

162. *Innocent until proven guilty.*
In a court of law, the accused person is presumed innocent at the start. The burden of proof always rests on the accuser, not the accused. The jury will not convict the person unless the proof is clear.

163. *Finders keepers, losers weepers.*
This saying is used to justify keeping what has been found in a public place. (Not all Americans consider this to be just. Many who find things either leave them alone or take them to a "lost and found" office if one is nearby.)

164. *Possession is nine-tenths of the law.*
A lawsuit will frequently go in favor of the person who currently has the disputed item. For example, if two brothers are disputing which of them inherited the house of their father, the one who is living in the house is more likely to win the case.

Human rights are the standard of American justice. Whatever protects human rights is just; whatever goes against human rights is unjust. Every American of whatever status has many personal rights, guaranteed by the "Bill of Rights" in the Constitution. These include such things as the right to speak one's mind in public (even if this insults the government), the right to worship as one pleases, the right to hold meetings with other citizens, and the right to own and carry weapons. People are expected not to violate each other's rights.

When people's rights are violated, they are expected to react strongly enough to stop the injustice. Sometimes it may also be fair for them to inflict a punishment or ask for some compensation for the injustice that was done to them. *Turnabout is fair play* (158).

Personal rights and freedoms go as far as they can without reducing the rights and freedoms of others. Laws about cigarette smoking are a clear example. For years it was presumed that if a smoker wanted to take the health risks of smoking, that was his or her free decision. According to recent research, nonsmokers may get cancer and other health problems if they are often inside a place where other people smoke. In other words, smoking in such a place is unjust and unfair to the nonsmoker. Now smoking is prohibited in many public places and workplaces.

The abortion debate deals with a similar issue. Does the free choice of a pregnant woman to have an abortion take away a "right" of the fetus? Religious conservatives believe that human rights start before the child is even born. The "right to life" (or the right to be born) is the first "human right." It is unjust to take that right away. In fact, it looks like murder, or something very close to murder.

Those who favor abortion say that human rights begin only at birth. To pass a law that restricts the woman's free choice in order to protect the "choice" of a fetus seems completely unjust to them. It is no accident that this movement does not call itself "proabortion" but "prochoice." Choice is the issue. A mother can make a choice; a fetus cannot. Therefore justice is thought to be on the side of the mother's choice.

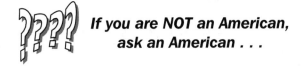

**If you are NOT an American,
ask an American . . .**

- When did something bother you so much that you said to yourself, *Enough is enough*? What did you do to change it?

DANGER

If you ARE an American,
watch out for cross-cultural trouble here

Our culture's ideas of justice rest on two principles that put power into the hands of the ordinary person — *Justice is blind* (161) and *The customer is always right* (51). In many other cultures, justice always has both eyes wide open (to the social status of the person concerned) and the one who is always right is the government, not the customer.

As we encounter rampant injustice in other countries, we may wonder why the local people do not rise up and say, *Enough is enough* (154). Quite simply, they have no Bill of Rights. They have never had one, and their government may be dedicated to the proposition that they will never get one. Even if they have a revolution, it rarely brings with it a revolution in thinking about the nature of government, as the American Revolution did. Soon the revolutionary liberators become the new oppressors and intimidators, as happens too often.

Credit and Blame

165. *You can lead a horse to water, but you can't make him drink.*

    Even when given an opportunity, some people will not use it. In that case, the blame is all on them.

166. *The devil made me do it.*

    I am not to blame for what I did. I could not help it. Some power outside of me was forcing me to act in that way. This is playfully used as an excuse by people who know they have done something wrong but want to avoid the penalty. It does not mean they really believe a devil exists or has any influence over their choices.

167. *If the shoe fits, wear it.*

    If an accusation is true, accept the blame. (This saying can also mean, "If a suitable opportunity comes to you, take it.")

168. *You made the bed, you lie in it.*

    You created a certain situation, so you are now responsible to take the consequences.

169. *Crime does not pay.*

    Though crime appears to have benefits, this is an illusion. For example, shoplifting seems like an easy way to get things one wants, but crime always puts the criminal in danger of punishment. This saying is a warning to those who foolishly think they will never be caught. This view is changing. One even hears the cynical opposite of this saying, *Crime pays.*

170. *Be sure your sins will find you out.*

    Same as previous proverb. Cover-ups do not work. The way to live is to do nothing you will later have to try to cover up.

171. *Chickens come home to roost.*

    Same as previous two proverbs. As chickens go home in the evening, so the results of wrongdoing come back on a person's own head at the appointed time. This may be said of someone who has gotten away with doing wrong for a while but now is obviously having to pay for it.

172. *The pot calling the kettle black.*

    Since the pot and the kettle are equally black from the cooking fire, the pot has no right to criticize the kettle. This might be used if someone known to be a gossip criticizes someone else for gossiping.

173. *Get a life.*

    Do not be so unreasonably critical about tiny things. Find something better to do with your time.

174. *There are two sides to everything.*

    Never assume that all the blame for a conflict lies on one side, especially if you have heard only one side of the story.

In matters of taking credit or passing blame, we again want to *have our cake and eat it too* (59). If we succeed at something, we want to take credit for it. If we fail, we want to find someone else to blame. In other words, we want to accept full responsibility for the good things and accept no responsibility for the bad ones. This protects our self-esteem.

Several proverbs remind us that this will not work. Each individual really is responsible for her actions. *You made the bed, you lie in it* (168). *Crime does not pay* (169); on the contrary, justice means that a person will have to pay for his crimes. No individual can escape this responsibility before the law of the land, regardless of personal status, wealth, or power. *Justice is blind* (161) to such things.

Though we do not like to take responsibility for our own actions, we love to demand that other people take responsibility for theirs. If their action hurts us in any way, we make them pay. Americans sue (and win) over matters that would get laughed out of court in most countries. In one well-known case, a woman sued a restaurant chain because they served her coffee so hot that it burned her badly when she spilled it in her own lap. The court awarded her almost half a million dollars in damages! No wonder there are almost a million lawyers in the United States.

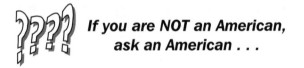

If you are NOT an American, ask an American . . .

- Why do Americans say, "The devil made me do it," if they don't believe there is a devil?

- What do you do to protect yourself from being sued? Have you ever been sued or considered suing someone else? What was the problem?

- My book says that a woman got half a million dollars when she sued a restaurant for burns from coffee she spilled in her own lap. In my country no one would dare to file a suit like that. Do you think suing over something like that is a sign of a healthy country or a sick one? Why?

DANGER

If you ARE an American, watch out for cross-cultural trouble here

Our cultural bias toward solving problems and improving things has some dangerous implications in the area of credit and blame. We tend to call attention to the individual who is responsible for a success or failure.

This is a gaffe in cultures that go to great lengths to avoid shame of any kind. We want to say, *If the shoe fits, wear it.* They would rather say, *If the shoe would fit (if an accusation is true), don't put your foot into it and let people see that it fits.*

In such cultures calling attention to a blameworthy act may be judged to be worse than the act itself. It takes a long time for a foreigner to learn the proper times and ways to assign blame, much longer than most Americans want to invest.

Authorities and Rules

When self-esteem, self-development, self-expression, and freedom of choice are core values in a culture, authorities and rules do not fit easily into the cultural pattern. We have already seen several proverbs that imply that each individual is his or her own authority. For example, *If it feels good, do it* (53); *Just do it* (86); *Live and let live* (47), and *To each his own* (48). There are also proverbs that directly mention authorities and rules.

175. *Rules are made to be broken (Commandment 8).*
Rules are not to be blindly and absolutely followed. Wise people will always ask themselves whether this rule really holds in this case. If it does not, they will break the rule in order to do what appears best at this particular time.

176. *There is an exception to every rule.*
Same as previous proverb.

177. *The exception proves the rule.*
Contrast to previous two proverbs. This could be stated as follows: "Though we are making an exception and breaking the rule in this one case, we do it only because the circumstances are so unusual. This proves that in normal circumstances the rule should be obeyed."

178. *The voice of the people is the voice of God.*
The ultimate authority in a society is found in the consensus of the average people.

179. *Power corrupts.*
Do not trust a person who has been in power for very long. When people are put into positions of power, they gradually forget what life is like for ordinary people. They become more likely to abuse their power, perhaps without even realizing it.

180. *The devil can quote scripture.*
A quotation from an authoritative book or person cannot always be trusted. The quote may be distorted or

incorrectly applied. The saying comes from the biblical story of the temptation of Jesus, in which the devil quoted some scripture to Jesus but twisted its meaning to suit his purpose.

In many cultures, proverbs remind people to trust and respect authorities of all kinds. By contrast, American proverbs teach people to question and challenge authorities. Our nation was born in a revolution that threw off an unwanted authority, and we have been throwing off authority ever since. Many of us do not want to deny all authority by saying, *If it feels good, do it* (53). Yet we each want to be our own authority with as little limitation as possible from other authorities in government, society, family, and the workplace. We see authorities as people who interfere with personal freedom.

We know that there must be some authorities in order for a nation to exist, but we insist that the basis for their authority is the consensus of the common people. *The voice of the people is the voice of God* (178). When the American people have spoken, as they do in an election, their word is the final authority. It is as if God himself has spoken. No one can challenge it, no matter how high an office one may hold. America has never had a military government.

American skepticism about authorities is also true of rules. Many cultures have proverbs that appreciate rules as good things. They are guides to right behavior. By contrast, most Americans see rules as limits to freedom. The fewer rules, the better.

In fact, we do not even like to quote proverbs in a way that makes them sound like rules. Instead we often stand them on their heads to show we do not believe them anymore. For example, the old saying *Winning isn't everything* (80) becomes *Winning isn't everything, it's the only thing. Crime does not pay* (169) becomes *Crime pays.* Or we change *Flattery will get you nowhere* (13) to *Flattery will get you everywhere.* The person who can question authority is more respected than the one who submits to authority without thinking.

We want to know the reason for every rule, and if the reason does not look obvious and necessary to us, we may say, *Rules are made to be broken* (175). For example, if a child asks a parent, "Why can't I do that?" and the parent replies, "Because I said so," the child does not accept this. If the parent gives no explanation, the child does not see any authority in the command. In other words, the child is the real "authority." The child will decide whether the parent's explanation is good enough to justify the rule.

One may ask how a culture of this type can get an army to function. Only with serious indoctrination during basic training! Recruits have to unlearn some of their most basic cultural values about self-esteem, questioning authority, and thinking for themselves.

They have to accept that military life has a completely different view of authority than civilian life. Though military people do not change completely, the process is made somewhat easier by the fact that for about a generation the military has been entirely made up of volunteers. The nation has not been exercising its authority to require individual citizens to do national service.

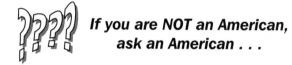

**If you are NOT an American,
ask an American . . .**

- If American children are taught to question every authority, including parents and teachers, when and how
do they learn to accept authority? How did you learn to
accept authority?

- Americans say, *Rules are made to be broken*, yet most
of the time you obey rules. How do you decide which
rules to keep and which ones to break?

 **DANGER**

**If you ARE an American,
watch out for cross-cultural trouble here**

Since we rarely hesitate to question authorities and rules in
America, we take the same approach when we enter other
cultures. If a local cultural rule does not make sense to us, we
either break it or we ask for an explanation. If we ask, we
are implying that those we are asking owe us an explanation
and we have a right to break the rule unless they can give us
a good one.

It does not come naturally to us to obey local cultural rules
that make no sense to us. A basic challenge of cultural adjust-
ment is the challenge to obey first and ask questions later.

Conflicts

181. *It takes two to make a quarrel.*
Avoid a fight if you can. An insult does not become a fight unless it is answered by an insult.

182. *Let a sleeping dog lie.*
Do not meddle in something that will cause you no trouble if you leave it alone. If you wake up the "dog," it may bite you.

183. *The pen is mightier than the sword.*
A conflict may be resolved more deeply and effectively by writing the truth than by resorting to violence.

184. *People who live in glass houses should not throw stones.*
Do not attack anyone if you have no way to defend yourself when they attack you in the same way. (The "glass houses" symbolize something that cannot be defended.)

185. *Sticks and stones may break my bones, but words will never hurt me.*
A taunt used by people claiming that an insult did not affect them.

186. *If you can't stand the heat, get out of the kitchen.*
Withdraw from an activity if you do not like the conflict and criticism it brings. Let other people do it without you.

187. *Opposites attract.*
As positive and negative magnets attract each other, so people of very different types attract each other. For example, a quiet woman marries a very outgoing man, or

vice versa. These differences have a mixed effect on the couple, partly making them interested in each other but also leading to miscommunication and conflict.

188. *He who laughs last, laughs best.*
If a person does wrong to someone and laughs at him or her, the victim will look for a way to get revenge. When revenge is taken, the victim *gets the last laugh,* defeating the other person.

189. *Don't get mad, get even.*
Similar to the previous proverb. When someone treats you badly, do not just get angry. Express your anger in action.

190. *Revenge is sweet.*
Similar to the previous two proverbs.

191. *Forgive and forget.*[3]
Opposite of previous three proverbs. Conflicts should be resolved and ended, not left alone to cause years of regret, bitterness, and pain.

192. *Let bygones be bygones.*
This is similar to the previous proverb. Do not bring up an old problem. Pretend it never happened. ("Bygones" are things that have "gone by," that is, things that are over.)

193. *Time heals all wounds.*
The damage done by a conflict is like a wound that will heal naturally over time if it is not reinjured.

---

3. See also *To err is human* (113).

Some degree of conflict is normal in life and can be handled in healthy ways. Conflict helps people learn how to stand up for themselves, which is very important in an individualistic society. Since *opposites attract* (187), human relationships are ambiguous, moving back and forth between enjoyment and conflict.

On the other hand, Americans do not enjoy conflict for its own sake. The proverb *It takes two to make a quarrel* (181) advises people to avoid conflict if possible. So do *Let a sleeping dog lie* (182) and *The pen is mightier than the sword* (183). Americans tend to avoid discussion of religion and politics because they believe such discussion can easily lead to conflicts.

Words, especially "fighting words," are often the trigger for conflict. When an insult comes, one may try to deflect it by saying, *The pot is calling the kettle black* (172), that is, "You have no right to criticize me. You are just as guilty as I am." Or you may reply to an insult with a threat such as, *People who live in glass houses should not throw stones* (184). Or, you may deny that the insult hurt you — *Sticks and stones may break my bones, but words will never hurt me* (185).

Because asserting individual rights is highly valued, violent conflict is common. "Road rage" is one of the most frightening new forms of violence. This term refers to one driver attacking another on the highway because of the way he was driving. Sometimes one driver may even shoot and kill another one. Why? It is a matter of personal dignity. He thinks this way: "I am just as important as anyone on the road. That driver was treating me like a piece of dirt. I had to show him that he cannot get away with that. *Enough is enough*" (154).

Though Americans believe in protecting our personal dignity and we say, *Revenge is sweet* (190), we are not at all sympathetic to this kind of violence. Unless the accused murderer can show he acted in self-defense, he will be convicted and imprisoned for years, perhaps even for life.

The gentler side of American values says, *Forgive and forget* (191), or *Let bygones be bygones* (192). Our optimism comes through in the proverb *Time heals all wounds* (193). Americans have a hard time understanding international tensions that have lasted for centuries. Perhaps this is because America changes its friends and enemies fairly quickly. Half a century ago, the Soviet Union was an ally with America against Germany; then it became the archenemy and (West) Germany became the friend. Now Russia and Germany are both allies against the new enemy, global terrorism.

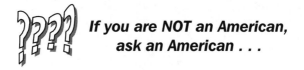 **If you are NOT an American, ask an American . . .**

- Do you generally avoid talking about religion and politics in order to avoid conflict with other people? Can you explain that for me? People in my country love to argue about those things.

- How do you explain road rage? Does it indicate anything about America in general, or is it only a few crazy people doing it?

 **DANGER**

If you ARE an American,
watch out for cross-cultural trouble here

If you live in another culture, the chances that you will get involved in some conflict with a local person or group are very high. So are the chances that you will handle it badly if you try to use American rules for interpersonal conflicts.

Each culture has its own patterns for handling conflict. Which grievances are so bad that they normally lead to conflict? Who argues with whom under what circumstances? What actions are expected and tolerated in a conflict? What groups get involved in carrying on or resolving a conflict between individuals?

If you can *let a sleeping dog lie*, that is the most prudent course. Sometimes that option is not open to you, as in a case where a local person takes offense because of some comment or action that you did not intend as an insult. If that happens, don't protest your innocence. You were only innocent by American standards. Ask for some advice so you can avoid repeating the cultural mistake.

Chapter Nine

Time and Change

. . . .

Time and Efficiency

If Americans are obsessed with anything, that thing is time. The view of time as a scarce, valuable thing affects all of American life. You are very likely to hear American sayings about time, such as the following:

194. *Time is money (Commandment 9).*
     Time can be converted to money, that is, wages are often paid per hour of work. Managers want employees to do things quickly because "time is money." If employees waste time, the company loses money.

195. *Making every minute count.*
     Doing something productive all the time. Not letting any time "slip away."

196. *Time flies.*
     One must hurry through life because each moment flies by, never to be retrieved. There is never enough time.

197. *Time's a-wasting.*
     This means, "Hurry up. Why are you still waiting to get started?"

198. *The sooner the better.*
A wish for quick action or quick change. Once a decision has been made, there is no point in waiting to carry it out.

199. *No time like the present.*
Do it now. Why wait?

200. *Now or never.*
Similar to previous proverb. Act now; you may not have another chance.

201. *Opportunity only knocks once.*[1]
Similar to previous two proverbs. Opportunity is like an unexpected stranger passing by. It knocks on someone's door. If the person fails to answer the door, opportunity goes away and knocks on someone else's door. It does not return to the same person.

202. *Make hay while the sun shines.*
Similar to previous three proverbs. If you do not seize the opportunity, rain may come and spoil the hay before you get into the barn.

203. *He who hesitates is lost.*
Similar to previous four proverbs.

204. *Business and pleasure don't mix.*
When you work, work. When you play, play. It is inefficient and therefore unwise to try to mix the two.

---

1. See also *You only go around once in life* (54) and *You are only young once* (121).

205. *The early bird catches the worm.*
Punctuality is important. If you want to succeed, arrive early, like the bird that hunts worms at dawn before they go into hiding for the day.

206. *Early to bed and early to rise makes a man healthy, wealthy, and wise.*
Similar to previous proverb.

207. *Make it short and sweet.*
Speak briefly and to the point. We do not have time for the details.

208. *Haste makes waste.*
Though acting quickly is generally a good thing, acting too quickly may cause trouble. This proverb is used when someone has done a job carelessly and wrongly. For example, a carpenter in a hurry may cut a board too short and have to throw it away.

209. *Better late than never.*
Though being on time is better than being late, doing something late is better than giving up and doing nothing.

Life is seen as an hourglass in which the days slip by like grains of sand until one's time is up. Life is not seen as an accumulation, an unfolding, a growth. It is a race, a race against time, and the human being always loses.

What is true of a lifetime is also true of each day, hour, and minute. Americans are time-conscious to an extreme. Next to the credit card, the watch is our worst slave-driver. We say, *Time is money* (194), and that means we never have enough of it. This view of time accounts for the very high level of stress in American life today.

If we think of time as a financial asset, we think we should work longer hours in order to get more money, even though this reduces the amount of time we have for pleasure and family. We start to calculate, "If I work this Saturday, I can make an extra $250. If I take the day off to go fishing with my son I will not get that money. So I will work, give my son $50 to go somewhere with his friends, and I will have $200 left."

When we say *Time is money* (194), we are almost saying, "Life is money" (though there is no such proverb). Since time is limited and lost opportunities are gone forever, one has to go through life *making every minute count* (195). That means one is always busy doing something (work or play) or experiencing something. We schedule everything, including our play. Then we say our schedules are so full that we need a vacation, but even on a "vacation" we try to pack in as many experiences as we can. We joke about getting home and having to recover from our vacation.

American life is lived in compartments, which are thought to make everything more efficient. *Business and pleasure don't mix* (204). During working time, a person is expected to work, not to joke, relax, sleep, or engage in long conversations that have nothing to do with work. During "pleasure" or "play" time, a person is expected not to do anything related to work.

Time spent sitting and reflecting does not count for much. In fact, silence makes Americans nervous. We no longer believe that silence is golden, that is, silence is of great value. We will do something to fill up the silence, usually switch on a

TV or radio just to have some noise in the background. There is always music playing in American stores and even during "moments of silence" in many American churches.

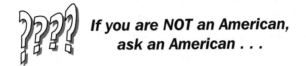

If you are NOT an American, ask an American . . .

- Americans seem to be obsessed with time, *making every minute count.* How does that attitude improve the quality of life and how does it reduce it?

- Do most Americans think they are too busy? If so, how did they get that way? Why do they stay that way?

- My book says that Americans do not think that sitting and reflecting on life is very important. Do you agree? When do you sit in silence and reflect? What do you think about?

DANGER

If you ARE an American, watch out for cross-cultural trouble here

When we go into another culture to work for a few weeks or even a few years, our short time frame and our success orientation guarantee that we will be out of step with what is happening there. In our minds, the dates of our arrival and departure in the country are crucial boundary markers. What happens between those dates has to be a success, or our self-esteem will take a beating.

We soon discover that no local people are on our schedule. Then we have a choice to make, perhaps the one most fundamental choice for Americans abroad. Will we stick with our schedule, pulling as many local people into it as we can, or will we switch to their time frame?

Their time frame may have a different idea of a work week, a different view of deadlines, a different annual cycle, and certainly not the same "finish line" as our time frame does. These differences are some of the heaviest pieces of American cultural baggage we subconsciously carry along with us.

Everything Changes

210. *Time marches on.*[2]

Time is marching to its own drumbeat. It does not slow down or stop for anyone.

211. *The worm turns.*[3]

Everything changes. Do not expect situations or people to stay the same for very long.

212. *Here today, gone tomorrow.*

Things may change quickly. This is said as a criticism of a person who changes quickly for no good reason. It may also be said of a thing or situation that does not last. Change is not good when it indicates unreliability.

Americans have very few traditions of any kind, except for three important holidays. Christmas, for many, involves gift

---

2. See also *Time and tide wait for no man* (232).
3. See also *What goes around comes around* (156).

exchanges with relatives and friends. Thanksgiving is a turkey dinner for the extended family. The Fourth of July involves a picnic and fireworks, celebrating our national independence.

Many traditions common in other countries are not found in America at all. There is no American national costume or dress, no influential American folk tales or myths, no standard American way to conduct weddings or funerals, no royal family, and (by comparison with many other cultures) not very many folk songs, proverbs, and sayings. We do not even have an official national language.

We live in a society where everything can change, and almost everything does. We expect it to. *Time marches on* (210). There are new styles of clothing, new hit songs, maybe a new job or even a new spouse. We elect a new president. We open a new highway, a new mall, and a new housing development.

We do not mind the changes. After all, success is a change. If we want to be more successful than we are now, something will have to change. Our whole lives are focused on how to get the right changes to happen, not on how to preserve something from changing.

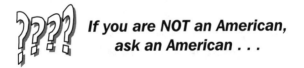

**If you are NOT an American,
ask an American . . .**

- What are the biggest changes you have made in your life?

- My country has lots of traditions, and they give our lives meaning. Traditions do not seem to be very important in America, and I don't quite understand where American life gets its meaning without them. Can you help me?

Change Is Usually Progress

213. *A new broom sweeps clean.*
     A new person in power will change many things and improve the situation. Change is better than leaving things as they are.

214. *Tomorrow is another day* (or *Tomorrow is a new day*).
     No matter how bad things are right now, a person may hope for better prospects in the morning. New opportunities will come.

215. *The darkest hour is just before the dawn.*
     Similar to previous proverb.

216. *Will wonders never cease?*
     Said when someone has done something untypical of him or her and much better than was expected. It may also be used of a technological breakthrough.

In our thinking today, we Americans still sacrifice the past on the altar of the future, that is, our loyalty to traditions of the past is usually less important than our trust in the future. Though we may sometimes long for the good old days, we do not really want to go back to the time before cell phones and video games. The real glory years for the country and the world are thought to lie in the future.

We have a deep belief that *Tomorrow is another day* (214), and things are going to get better. Someone will find a cure for AIDS. Someone will find an inexpensive alternative for fossil fuel. Someone will invent a diet pill that works — *Will wonders never cease?* (216). The human beings of the next century will be stronger, smarter, and happier than people today. They will live in more energy-efficient houses, have cheaper and quicker access to far more information, eat better food, have better health and more leisure time, enjoy cleaner air, drive safer cars on better roads.

What is the basis for our faith in progress? Historically it has been faith in individual hard work and bright ideas, especially in the areas of science and technology. It does not rest on business, religion, human nature, God, or (least of all) government.

The "New Age" Movement is one type of faith in progress without much faith in people, God, or any other power. The basic "New Age" idea is that time progresses by itself in ages or eras. We are supposedly at the beginning of a "New Age" which will be much better than the last one. This is almost a faith in time itself. For some New Agers it is faith in the stars as the indicators of "ages" in history.

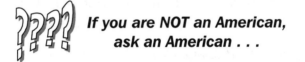

If you are NOT an American, ask an American . . .

- Is the world generally changing for the better or going downhill? Will technology make life much better for most people in the next generation?

- Some people think the world is coming into a "New Age." What do you know about the "New Age" view of life? Do you take that view seriously?

Change at a Deep Level Is Not Easy

217. *You can't teach an old dog new tricks.*
     Once habits are learned, it is very hard to change them.

218. *History repeats itself.*
There are patterns in history. Nations rise and fall for similar reasons. Nations do not change their ways or learn from the mistakes of others. They repeat them.

219. *The more things change, the more they stay the same.*
Said when an apparent change is only superficial. For example, if a dictator is overthrown by a liberator but after one year the liberator has turned into a new dictator, this proverb would apply.

220. *Nature abhors a vacuum.*
As air rushes back into a vacuum tube through the first crack in the tube, so life rushes to get back to the way it was before someone made a change. For example, a person cleans a stack of papers off a bedroom dresser, but a few days later there is a new stack in its place. The change was only superficial and temporary.

221. *The leopard cannot change his spots.*
Some people are not willing or able to change their character. This is said when a notoriously bad person tries to change but falls into the same mistake all over again.

Much as we like change, we know that some things are almost impossible to change. For example, we doubt that our government will ever do anything efficiently. Government is by nature bureaucratic, monopolistic, and nonprofit. All these characteristics go against American core values, including *time is money* (194). How then can government become efficient, no matter which people we put into government offices? Nevertheless, we keep trying to "change the system," "reinvent government," "reduce government paperwork," "reform the welfare system," replace our tax collection structure, etc. We try for small changes even when we despair about any big changes.

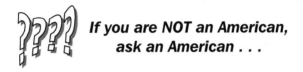

If you are NOT an American, ask an American . . .

- Do you usually vote in elections? Why or why not?

- You say, "History repeats itself." Does that mean it is a waste of time to try to change things?

 **DANGER**

If you ARE an American, watch out for cross-cultural trouble here

Since many Americans go overseas to promote change of some kind, they run head-on into change-resistant cultures. Some of these cultures are very old dogs that do not want to learn any new (American) tricks (see 217).

For example, an Indian friend once remarked to me, "For you Americans, a problem is something to solve. In India, a problem is something to live around." Americans who visit India are indeed astounded at the problems that Indians seem content and competent to live around, such as roads (and potholes) shared more or less equally by pedestrians, oxen, and all manner of wheeled vehicles.

Why don't they change? In fact, they do change a bit. The difference is that they do not expect to change, nor do they value change as Americans do. They simply do not believe that *Time marches on* (210). Time is not going anywhere. Like the hands of a watch, it keeps making circles, always coming back to where it was.

Chapter Ten

Hope and God

. . . .

Optimism

In chapter 2, "The Top Priority in American Life," we saw that Americans take risks confidently and work with determination in spite of setbacks. In chapter 9, "Time and Change," we saw the American belief that changes are usually improvements. This optimism is also clear in the following more general proverbs.

222. *Look on the bright side.*
     Try to see the good side of a difficult situation. Keep your hopes up.

223. *Every cloud has a silver lining.*
     Even bad situations will contain something good if we look for it. Clouds are considered symbols of undesirable things. The bright edge of a dark cloud is like something good that can cheer us up.

224. *Half a loaf is better than no bread at all.*
     Sometimes we will not be able to get all we want or hope for. At such times of only partial success, we should *Look on the bright side* (222) and be glad for what we got.

225. *No news is good news.*

If a friend is traveling and one does not hear from her, one may assume that everything is going well. If she had run into a problem or had an accident, surely she would have telephoned. As another proverb says, *Bad news travels fast.*

226. *Lightning never strikes twice in the same place.*

It seems unfair that the same strange and unexpected calamity would fall twice on the same person. This may be used to encourage a person who has been struck by tragedy and is constantly worrying that another tragedy may come.

These proverbs represent an underlying American cultural belief that we should be positive about life, even the parts of life that seem difficult. If we *look on the bright side* (222), we are more likely to keep trying for success. Though we never like to settle for a partial success, *Half a loaf is better than no bread at all* (224). Perhaps we can get the other half of the loaf later.

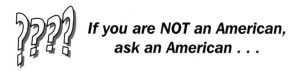

If you are NOT an American, ask an American . . .

- What is so good about being optimistic? Is there any difference between optimism and wishful thinking? Isn't it more sensible to be realistic?

- If American influence were greater overseas, would the world be a better place? What do you think would change?

DANGER

If you ARE an American, watch out for cross-cultural trouble here

Much of the rest of the world, particularly Europe, has a love-hate relationship with American optimism and enthusiasm. On the one hand they admire us for what we are willing to tackle and how ready we are to believe we can change it. On the other hand they consider us very naïve to imagine that our efforts will do much good.

Europeans know that we tend to overstate the benefits we expect from our new ideas and underestimate the costs. Unlike us, they respect the language of understatement but are turned off by anything that sounds like American hype.

God, Spiritual Power, and Destiny

227. *God helps those who help themselves (Commandment 10).*
     God looks favorably on people who take initiative. If you want something, work for it.

228. *In God we trust.*
     This motto is clearly displayed on every American coin and bill. It means many different things to different Americans. A few would even like to get rid of it.

229. *God bless America.*
     This prayer is also the title of a song often sung on patriotic occasions. Some politicians use it as the final line in a speech, especially when the issue is war.

230. *Marriages are made in heaven.*

God is the source of human love and the One who destines two individuals to be married. This proverb is going out of fashion since it goes against individual freedom. Sometimes it is still used to refer to a merger of two companies that seems to work to the advantage of both.

231. *What will be will be.*

Some things cannot be changed or avoided.

232. *Time and tide wait for no man.*

Similar to previous proverb. When something's time has come, it will happen and nothing can stop it. It is like an ocean tide coming in to the shore.

233. *The good die young.*

Life is not always fair. Some very fine people die at a young age though it seems they were so good they deserved to live longer.

234. *Man proposes, God disposes.*

Human beings make their plans, but God determines whether they succeed or not.

235. *You can't fool Mother Nature.*

There are natural laws which humans cannot change. Planting seeds in autumn will not fool Mother Nature into thinking it is spring. ("Mother Nature" is just a vague term for the natural world and the processes by which it functions. Most Americans see nature as an impersonal thing. We do not think of Mother Nature as an earth goddess.)

In many parts of the world, America is seen as a "Christian country." By comparison with most European countries, America is indeed very religious; however, in America all religion is unofficial. Americans hold to a long-established tradition of the "separation of church and state." As English is the most used language but has never been established as America's official language, so Christianity is the most widespread religion but has never been established as the official religion.

Our money is all marked with the phrase *In God we trust* (228), but as a nation we never say which "God" we are talking about or what we mean by "trusting" God. We have no common proverbs that describe the greatness of God or instruct people to respect God. The few who mention God do not give him much credit for anything. For example, we have already noted, *The voice of the people is the voice of God* (178).

A similar idea is found in the saying *God helps those who help themselves* (227). It can mean either that God will bless those who take initiative or that God is not a factor in how things turn out. The idea is that if one merely sits and prays but takes no actions, nothing good will happen.

It may appear that in America the real "god" (the ultimate center of attention and devotion) is the individual. Even many of the religious Americans try to get God to revolve around us, rather than adjusting our lives to revolve around him. We want God to meet our individual needs. We are not so interested in fitting into his master plan for the universe. The vast majority of us Americans say we believe in God, but, crudely stated, many of us want to use God rather than worship him.

A few Americans even give up on believing in God at all. If *the good die young* (233), Americans want an explanation. Is God trying to do anything to prevent the deaths of good people at a young age? If he is trying, why isn't he succeeding? Even Americans who believe in God take these questions seriously. A best-selling book by a religious teacher has the title *When Bad Things Happen to Good People*. A nation that worships success cannot worship a God who fails.

There are very few common proverbs about gods and goddesses, angels,[1] demons,[2] or the spirits of the dead, but that is less surprising since all those are far less prominent in American religion than God himself. Proverbs about impersonal forces such as destiny, fate, or history[3] are also few. They are far outweighed by the proverbs on individual initiative.

Americans want to believe that anything is possible through individual effort. We do not believe that fate, God, or any other unseen power has determined things and left us powerless to change them. We do not often say anymore, *What will be will be* (231), *Time and tide wait for no man* (232), or *Man proposes, God disposes* (234).

As we have seen in the section on optimism, we have almost limitless faith in our own ability to change things for the better. Many Americans think God will help us change things, but sometimes it looks like our faith in ourselves is greater than our faith in God. And when we succeed, we want to claim most of the credit.

---

1. See *Fools rush in where angels fear to tread* (106).
2. See *Better the devil you know than the devil you don't* (117), *The devil made me do it* (166), and *Idle hands are the devil's workshop* (93).
3. See *History repeats itself* (218).

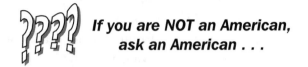

If you are NOT an American,
ask an American . . .

- When you say, *God helps those who help themselves*, does that mean that you believe God really does help them or you don't believe God does anything, so people had better do things for themselves?

- Why has "God Bless America" been sung so much ever since the World Trade Center was destroyed? Did Americans think about God anymore or any differently after that attack?

- My book says, "It may appear that the real 'god' in America is the individual person." What do you think that means? How true do you think it is?

 **DANGER**

If you ARE an American,
watch out for cross-cultural trouble here

Like Europeans, most Americans regard religious experience and practice as a private matter of personal preference, not much related to the rest of ordinary life. We assume other cultures keep (or should keep) the same separation between religion and life, but in fact other cultures often weave them together very closely.

In more religious cultures we need to ask people questions that we rarely ask other Americans. Which unseen powers do they believe exist? What effect do these powers have on life, health, work, family, etc.? Why is it important for everyone in a culture to belong to the same religion? What is the proper relationship between religion and politics?

This last question is particularly urgent with respect to America's relation to the Islamic world since Islam is the largest religion that believes its requirements should be made into law and enforced by the political establishment wherever possible. Most Americans say that Islam is wrong about this. We claim that religion should be a personal matter, but in times of war or terrorism we turn around and sing, "God Bless America." This is not an easy contradiction to explain to our foreign friends.

Conclusion

Like all cultures, American culture has some great strengths, some glaring weaknesses, and some strange paradoxes. It may be too simplistic to conclude that Americans are lonely superachievers, but there is some truth to that. We try to get everything without giving up anything, but it seems *you can't have your cake and eat it too* (59).

Success, self-esteem, and fun appear to be the most highly valued things in our culture. Love, money, and "playing to win" are valued nearly as highly. Personal freedom and personal initiative make it possible for Americans to pursue these values.

While we are *looking out for number one* (49), we give less attention to group loyalty, family relationships, and sexual morality. All these tend to put limits on the individual pursuit of the primary values. As for God and fate, they get some attention, but when they conflict with core cultural values, the core values usually take priority.

American culture is changing rapidly in areas such as gender roles, where there is no agreement about what is proper and desirable. It is hard to know what the next generation will do with the culture they inherit. It seems that they may be less achievement-oriented and more people-oriented than their parents. They certainly have more options, more money, more free time, and more teaching on self-esteem than any previous generation. How can it be that so many of them are still bored, aimless, and taking drugs? *If we're so rich, why ain't we smart?* (contrast 71).

American culture assumes that if a society creates opportunities for its youth, everything else will turn out right. That assumption is not standing up well. America has not yet determined what else it needs or where else it should look. If America changes this basic assumption, the effects will permeate and transform the whole culture, but in what direction? We do not know. We cannot find direction in sayings like *Just do it* (86) or *Go for it* (14). They don't even tell us what "it" is.

America has vast wealth, power, and influence. It may be the best country in the world for shopping, having fun, or making your life a success. But is it the best country for "living"? Are we the freest people in the world and yet voluntary slaves to the clock and the credit card? Is consumerism the key to the good life or the start of the rat race? Is the whole American Dream *too good to be true?* (25) *Time will tell* (30).

Reading List

Althen, Gary. *American Ways: A Guide for Foreigners in the United States*, 2nd ed. Yarmouth, Maine: Intercultural Press, 2002. Once you have covered the "ABCs" of American culture, this may be the best book to take you on to the "DEFs" and the rest of the alphabet. Intercultural Press publishes numerous books in this field, including several that compare American culture with one other culture.

Collis, Harry. *101 American English Proverbs: Understanding Language and Culture through Commonly Used Sayings*. Lincolnwood, Ill.: Passport Books, 1992. Cartoons and conversational examples make this an easy and enjoyable introductory book. (Note: Of the 101 proverbs in Collis's book, 61 are also used here in *American Cultural Baggage*.)

Engel, Dean. *Passport USA: Your Pocket Guide to American Business, Customs, and Etiquette*. San Rafael, Calif.: World Trade Press, 1997. See especially pages 14–30 on American values and behavior patterns.

Hirsch, E. D., et al. *The Dictionary of Cultural Literacy*. 2nd ed. Boston: Houghton Mifflin, 1993. See pages 47–58 on proverbs.

Kim, Eun Y. *The Yin and Yang of American Culture: A Paradox*. Yarmouth, Maine: Intercultural Press, 2001. An extremely helpful description and critique of the positive (yang) and negative (yin) sides of American culture, with suggestions from an Asian perspective for Americans in a global era.

Lanier, Sarah A. *Foreign to Familiar: A Guide to Understanding Hot- and Cold-Climate Cultures*. Hagerstown, Md.: McDougal

Publishing, 2000. A highly readable description of seven key contrasts between the American and European (cold-climate) cultures and the hot-climate cultures further south.

Lau, Kimberly J. " 'It's about Time': The Ten Proverbs Most Frequently Used in Newspapers and Their Relation to American Values." *Proverbium: Yearbook of International Proverb Scholarship* 13 (1996): 141–59. An intriguing study based on a computerized search of American newspapers on the Internet. The article includes an alphabetical list of 315 common proverbs from Whiting's *Modern Proverbs and Proverbial Phrases*. Cambridge, Mass.: Harvard University Press, 1989.

Mieder, Wolfgang, Stewart Kingsbury, and Kelsie Harder. *A Dictionary of American Proverbs*. New York: Oxford University Press, 1992. Almost 15,000 proverbs, listed by key word. Many references cited. Helpful cross-references between proverbs.

Nussbaum, Stan. *Why Are Americans Like That? A Visitor's Guide to American Cultural Values and Expectations*. Colorado Springs, Colo.: Enculturation Books, 2005. An abridged version of *American Cultural Baggage*, omitting the material aimed at American readers and condensing the rest.

Stewart, Edward C., and Milton J. Bennett. *American Cultural Patterns: A Cross-Cultural Perspective*. Yarmouth, Maine: Intercultural Press, 1991. Perhaps the best analytical overview of the subject. Excellent bibliography for further study.

Titelman, Gregory Y. *Random House Dictionary of America's Popular Proverbs and Sayings*. 2nd ed. New York: Random House, 2000.

Walmsley, Jane. *Brit-Think, Ameri-Think*. New York: Viking Penguin, 1986. A witty and very insightful comparison of British and American culture. Though Britain and America have many proverbs in common, the two cultural patterns are worlds apart.

Alphabetical List of Proverbs

The numbers in the following list refer to the number of the proverb, not the number of the page on which it is found.

A bird in the hand is worth two in the bush, 33

A dog is a man's best friend, 138

A fool and his money are soon parted, 77

A friend in need is a friend indeed, 132

A good captain goes down with his ship, 135

A house divided against itself cannot stand, 140

A live dog is better than a dead lion, 133

A man is only as old as he feels, 122

A man may work from sun to sun, but woman's work is never done, 125

A man's home is his castle, 124

A new broom sweeps clean, 213

Absence makes the heart grow fonder, 68

Actions speak louder than words, 89

All that glitters is not gold, 24

Don't bite off more than you can chew, 36

Don't count your chickens before they are hatched, 34

Don't get mad, get even, 189

Don't put all your eggs in one basket, 32

Don't put the cart before the horse, 11

Early to bed and early to rise makes a man healthy, wealthy, and wise, 206

Easy come, easy go, 100

Easy does it, 12

Enough is enough (Commandment 7), 154

Every cloud has a silver lining, 223

Every little bit helps, 21

Finders keepers, losers weepers, 163

First come, first served, 104

Flattery will get you nowhere, 13

Fools rush in where angels fear to tread, 106

Forgive and forget, 191

Get a life, 173

Give him an inch and he'll take a mile, 105

Go for it, 14

God bless America, 229

God helps those who help themselves (Commandment 10), 227

Half a loaf is better than no bread at all, 224

Haste makes waste, 208

He who hesitates is lost, 203

He who laughs last, laughs best, 188

Here today, gone tomorrow, 212

Hindsight is always 20/20, 37

History repeats itself, 218

Home is where the heart is, 150

Home, sweet home, 148

Honesty is the best policy, 160

Idle hands are the devil's workshop, 93

If at first you don't succeed, try, try again, 45

If it ain't broke, don't fix it, 107

If it feels good, do it, 53

If the shoe fits, wear it, 167

If you can't beat 'em, join 'em, 7

If you can't stand the heat, get out of the kitchen, 186

If you scratch my back, I'll scratch yours, 131

If you want something done right, do it yourself, 95

If you're so smart, why ain't you rich? 71

In God we trust, 228

Innocent until proven guilty, 162

It isn't over till the fat lady sings, 42

It isn't whether you win or lose, it's how you play the game, 79

It takes two to make a quarrel, 181

It takes two to tango, 58

It's a woman's prerogative to change her mind, 126

Just do it (Commandment 5), 86

Justice is blind, 161

Keeping up with the Joneses, 120